First World War
and Army of Occupation
War Diary
France, Belgium and Germany

3 CAVALRY DIVISION
6 Cavalry Brigade
3rd Dragoon Guards (Prince of Wales' Own)
30 October 1914 - 31 January 1919

WO95/1153/2

The Naval & Military Press Ltd
www.nmarchive.com
Published in association with The National Archives

Published by

The Naval & Military Press Ltd

Unit 10 Ridgewood Industrial Park,

Uckfield, East Sussex,

TN22 5QE England

Tel: +44 (0) 1825 749494

www.naval-military-press.com

www.nmarchive.com

This diary has been reprinted in facsimile from the original. Any imperfections are inevitably reproduced and the quality may fall short of modern type and cartographic standards.

© **Crown Copyright**
Images reproduced by permission of The National Archives, London, England, 2015.

Contents

Document type	Place/Title	Date From	Date To
Heading	WO95/1153/2 3 Cavalry Division 6 Cavalry Brigade 3 Dragoon Guards Oct 1914-Jan 1919		
Heading	1914-1919 3rd Cavalry Division 6th Cavalry Brigade.3rd Dragoon Guard Oct 1914-Jan 1919		
Heading	6th Cavalry Brigade 3rd Dragoon Guards Vol I 30.10.14-4.1.15 Jan 1919		
War Diary	Ludgershall	30/10/1914	30/10/1914
War Diary	Southampton	31/10/1914	31/10/1914
War Diary	Le Havre	01/11/1914	02/11/1914
War Diary	Railway Journey	03/11/1914	03/11/1914
War Diary	Cassell	04/11/1914	04/11/1914
War Diary	No. 1 Camp	05/11/1914	05/11/1914
War Diary	Trenches Heronthage Wood	06/11/1914	07/11/1914
War Diary	No. 2 Camp	08/11/1914	12/11/1914
War Diary	Trenchs at Zillebeke	13/11/1914	13/11/1914
War Diary	No. 3 Camp	14/11/1914	14/11/1914
War Diary	No. 4 Camp	15/11/1914	15/11/1914
War Diary	Trenchs at Zillebeke	16/11/1914	17/11/1914
War Diary	Trenchs at Zillebeke	17/11/1914	17/11/1914
War Diary	No. 4 Camp	18/11/1914	20/11/1914
War Diary	Billets L'Epinette Caudescure District	21/11/1914	14/12/1914
War Diary	Billets Bailleul	15/12/1914	16/12/1914
War Diary	Billets L'Epinette Caudescure District	17/12/1914	04/01/1915
Heading	6th Cavalry Brigade 3rd Dragoon Guards Vol II 10-29.1.15		
War Diary	Billets L'Epinette Caudescure District	10/01/1915	28/01/1915
War Diary	Billets Boeseghem	29/01/1915	29/01/1915
Heading	6th Cavalry Brigade 3rd Dragoon Guards Vol III 2-25.2.15		
War Diary	Boeseghem	02/02/1915	03/02/1915
War Diary	Ypres	04/02/1915	04/02/1915
War Diary	1 mile S.E. of Zillebere	08/02/1915	13/02/1915
War Diary	Ypres	13/02/1915	13/02/1915
War Diary	Boeseghem	21/02/1915	25/02/1915
Heading	6th Cavalry Brigade 3rd Dragoon Guards Vol IV 2-31 2-15		
Heading	3rd (Prince Of Wales) Dragoon Guards		
War Diary	Boiseghem	02/03/1915	11/03/1915
War Diary	Merville	12/03/1915	14/03/1915
War Diary	Boeseghem	14/03/1915	31/03/1915
Heading	3rd Cavalry Brigade 3rd Dragoon Guards Vol V 1-30.4.15		
War Diary		01/04/1915	30/04/1915
Heading	3rd Cavalry Division 3rd Dragoon Guards Vol VI 1-30 5.15		
War Diary	Boeseghem	01/05/1915	30/05/1915
Heading	3rd Cavalry Division 3rd Dragoon Guards Part of Vol VII 3.1.15-5.6.15		
War Diary		31/05/1915	05/06/1915

Type	Description	Start	End
Heading	3rd Cavalry Division 3rd Dragoon Guards Vol VII 31.5-30.6.15		
War Diary		31/05/1915	30/06/1915
Heading	3rd Cavalry Division 3rd Dragoon Guards Vol VIII 1-31.7.15		
War Diary		01/07/1915	31/07/1915
Heading	3rd Cavalry Division 3rd Dragoon Guards Vol IX August 15		
War Diary		01/08/1915	31/08/1915
Diagram etc	Scale: One Inch To 1.58 Mile		
Heading	6th Cav. Bde. 3rd Cav. Div. War Diary 3rd Dragoon Guards September And October 1915		
War Diary		01/09/1915	27/09/1915
War Diary	RBA	01/10/1915	31/12/1915
Heading	3rd (P of W's) Dragoon Gds Period War Diary 3rd (pot ws) Dragoon Gds Period:- From Vol X to XI January to March 1916		
War Diary		01/01/1916	04/01/1916
War Diary	Sailly-La-Bourse	05/01/1916	06/01/1916
War Diary	Bethune	07/01/1916	10/01/1916
War Diary	Vermelles	11/01/1916	11/01/1916
War Diary	D1 Sector Front Line	12/01/1916	17/01/1916
War Diary	Bethune	18/01/1916	19/01/1916
War Diary	Offin	20/01/1916	31/03/1916
Heading	3rd Dragoon Guards. Appendices To War Diary		
Miscellaneous	Report of Operations Nov. 5th To 6th Appendix 1		
Miscellaneous	Operations 8th 9th Nov: Appendix II.		
Miscellaneous	Report on operations Nov. 12th 13th. Appendix III.		
Miscellaneous	Report on Operations. Appendix IV.		
Heading	War Diary 3rd Dragoon Guards Vol April 1916.3rd Dragoon Guards April 1916		
War Diary	Offin	01/04/1916	16/05/1916
War Diary	St Ricquier	17/05/1916	21/05/1916
War Diary	Offin	22/05/1916	24/05/1916
War Diary	Paris Plage	25/05/1916	06/06/1916
War Diary	Offin	07/06/1916	24/06/1916
War Diary	Marcheville	25/06/1916	25/06/1916
War Diary	Domart	26/06/1916	26/06/1916
War Diary	Bonnay	27/06/1916	04/07/1916
War Diary	Meerlesart	05/07/1916	16/07/1916
War Diary	Vaux-Sur Somme	16/07/1916	19/07/1916
War Diary	La Neuville	20/07/1916	31/07/1916
War Diary	La Mesge	01/08/1916	02/08/1916
War Diary	Caours	03/08/1916	03/08/1916
War Diary	Lamesge	01/08/1916	02/08/1916
War Diary	Caours	03/08/1916	04/08/1916
War Diary	Roussent	05/08/1916	05/08/1916
War Diary	Offin	06/08/1916	11/09/1916
War Diary	Argoules	11/09/1916	11/09/1916
War Diary	Le Plessiel	12/09/1916	12/09/1916
War Diary	La Chaussee	13/09/1916	13/09/1916
War Diary	N of Bussy	14/09/1916	14/09/1916
War Diary	W of Bonnay	15/09/1916	17/09/1916
War Diary	Pont Noyelles	18/09/1916	22/09/1916
War Diary	1 D Mesge	23/09/1916	23/09/1916
War Diary	Wavins	24/09/1916	24/09/1916

Type	Description	From	To
War Diary	Maintenay	25/09/1916	21/10/1916
War Diary	Campigneuilles Les-Grandes	22/10/1916	31/10/1916
Heading	3rd Dragoon Guards Nominal roll of all Officers W.O's, N. CO's and men serving with the Regiment on the 31-10-16, Who came to France with the Regiment in October 1914		
Miscellaneous	Regtl Headquarters 3rd Dragoon Gds		
Miscellaneous	A Squadron 3rd Dragoon Guards.		
Miscellaneous	B Squadron 3rd Dragoon Guards		
Miscellaneous	C Squadron 3rd Dragoon Gds		
War Diary	Berck Sands	01/11/1916	27/11/1916
War Diary	Bois De Verton	28/11/1916	29/11/1916
War Diary	Berck	30/11/1916	30/11/1916
Heading	War Diary 3rd Dragoon Guards December, 1916		
War Diary	Campigneulles-Les-Grandes	01/12/1916	19/12/1916
War Diary	Airon St Vaast	20/12/1916	31/12/1916
War Diary	AIX-En-ISSART	01/01/1917	33/04/1917
Miscellaneous	Operations of 3rd Dragoon Guards April 5th-11th 1917 Arras		
Miscellaneous	Report on Three Sections Of 6th Machine Gun Squadron Attached 3rd Dragoon Guards On April 11th 1917.	02/05/1917	02/05/1917
Miscellaneous	3rd Dragoon Guards Casualties 11th April 1917		
Miscellaneous	Recommendations Forwarded To Brigade Headquarters For Immediate Recognition. At Arras 11th April 1917	14/04/1917	14/04/1917
Miscellaneous	List of Officers Present During Operations 5th To 11th April 1917 About Monchy Le Preux And Arras.	14/04/1917	14/04/1917
Miscellaneous	List of Honours and Rewards (Recent Operations)		
War Diary	Petit Preux	01/05/1917	11/05/1917
War Diary	Dumpierre	12/05/1917	13/05/1917
War Diary	Berthecourt	14/05/1917	14/05/1917
War Diary	La-Neuville	15/05/1917	17/05/1917
War Diary	Harbonnieres	17/05/1917	19/05/1917
War Diary	Buire	20/05/1917	31/05/1917
War Diary	? Epehy Tombois Farm (Exclusive) The Catalet Co. R.E.	23/05/1917	03/06/1917
War Diary	Buire	01/06/1917	30/06/1917
Miscellaneous	Diary From 10th June 1917 to June 29th 1917	29/06/1917	29/06/1917
War Diary	Buire	01/07/1917	10/07/1917
War Diary	Marles Les Mines	11/07/1917	16/07/1917
War Diary	Le Corbie	17/07/1917	30/09/1917
War Diary	Le Sart	01/10/1917	19/10/1917
War Diary	Hestrus	20/10/1917	22/10/1917
War Diary	Vacquerie Le Bourcq	23/10/1917	23/10/1917
War Diary	Ribeaucourt	24/10/1917	24/10/1917
War Diary	Longpre	25/10/1917	16/11/1917
War Diary	Franvillers	17/11/1917	18/11/1917
War Diary	Cappy	19/11/1917	22/11/1917
War Diary	Herissart	23/11/1917	21/12/1917
War Diary	Ailly	22/12/1917	31/12/1917
War Diary	Ailly-Le-Haut Clocher	01/01/1918	28/01/1918
War Diary	Lachausee Marcelcave	29/01/1917	29/01/1917
War Diary	Tertry	30/01/1918	13/03/1918
War Diary	Devise	14/03/1917	21/03/1917
War Diary	Beaumont	22/03/1918	28/03/1918
War Diary	Chaisy Au Bac	29/03/1918	31/03/1918

Heading	6th Cav. Bde 3rd Cav. Div. War Diary 3rd Dragoon Guards. April 1918		
War Diary	Sains-En Amenois	01/04/1918	01/04/1918
War Diary	In the Field	02/04/1918	06/04/1918
War Diary	Camon	07/04/1918	11/04/1918
War Diary	Rougefay	12/04/1918	12/04/1918
War Diary	Epps	13/04/1918	13/04/1918
War Diary	Bailleul Les Pernes	14/04/1918	04/05/1918
War Diary	Bourbers	05/05/1918	05/05/1918
War Diary	Villers L'Hopital	06/05/1918	07/05/1918
War Diary	Contay	07/05/1918	17/05/1918
War Diary	Belloy	18/05/1918	31/05/1918
War Diary	Behencourt	01/06/1918	13/06/1918
War Diary	Belloy-Sur-Somme	14/06/1918	25/06/1918
War Diary	Le Mesge	26/06/1918	06/08/1918
War Diary	Field	07/08/1918	10/08/1918
War Diary	Fouencamps	11/08/1918	15/08/1918
War Diary	Le Mesge	16/08/1918	18/08/1918
Miscellaneous	3rd Dragoon Guards Diary of Operations August 8th to August 11th 1918. Appendix A		
War Diary	Frevent	01/09/1918	06/09/1918
War Diary	Wail	07/09/1918	25/09/1918
War Diary	Louvincourt	26/09/1918	26/09/1918
War Diary	Meaulte	27/09/1918	27/09/1918
War Diary	Hem	28/09/1918	29/09/1918
War Diary	Bihecourt	30/09/1918	12/10/1918
War Diary	Elincourt	13/10/1918	13/10/1918
War Diary	Bantouzelle	14/10/1918	14/10/1918
War Diary	Le Mesge	19/10/1918	21/10/1918
War Diary	Montrelet	22/10/1918	25/10/1918
War Diary	Le Ponchel	26/10/1918	26/10/1918
War Diary	Sericourt	27/10/1918	31/10/1918
War Diary	Manancourt	15/10/1918	31/10/1918
Miscellaneous	3/rd Dragoon Guards Narrative of events from September 23rd to Octr 12th 1918		
War Diary	Manancourt	01/11/1918	11/11/1918
War Diary	Fices	11/11/1918	11/11/1918
War Diary	Leuze	11/11/1918	11/11/1918
War Diary	Waulx	12/11/1918	12/11/1918
War Diary	Wasmes	13/11/1918	19/11/1918
War Diary	Hennueyeres	19/11/1918	21/11/1918
War Diary	Mont. St. Guibert.	21/11/1918	22/11/1918
War Diary	Hanret	23/11/1918	24/11/1918
War Diary	Dhuy	25/11/1918	10/12/1918
War Diary	Anthiet	11/12/1918	11/12/1918
War Diary	St. Georges	12/12/1918	31/12/1918
War Diary	St. Georges	01/01/1919	31/01/1919

②

WO 95/1153

3 Cavalry Division
6 Cavalry Brigade

3 Dragoon Guards

Oct 1914 – Jan 1919.

1914-1919
3RD CAVALRY DIVISION
6TH CAVALRY BRIGADE.

3RD DRAGOON GUARDS
OCT 1914 - JAN 1919

6th Cavalry Brigade/3

121/4042

3rd Dragoon Guards.

Vol I 30.10.14 — 4.1.15

Jan 1919

Army Form C. 2118.

Page 1

WAR DIARY
or
INTELLIGENCE SUMMARY
(Erase heading not required.)

Instructions regarding War Diaries and Intelligence Summaries are contained in F. S. Regs., Part II. and the Staff Manual respectively. Title pages will be prepared in manuscript.

Hour, Date, Place		Summary of Events and Information	Remarks and references to Appendices
30.10.14	LUDGERSHALL	Regt. left LUDGERSHALL STA. as follows for S'HAMPTON.- B Sqdn. 12.15 p.m. A 1.15 p.m. C 2.15 p.m. H.Q. 3.15. Regt. entrained at 8 p.m.	8.10.
31.10.14	SOUTHAMPTON.	Sailed 1 a.m. covered outside LE HAVRE 8.30 p.m.	8.10.
1.11.14	LE HAVRE.	Disembarked 6.30 A.M. marched to REST CAMP.	8.10.
2.11.14	LE HAVRE.	Sqdns. left Rest Camp at 1 hrs. intervals – entrained at Dock Sta. for front commencing with H.Q. C Sqdn. at 8 p.m.	8.10.
3.11.14	RAILWAY JOURNEY	Regt. arrived 12 m.n. at CASSELL. distributed – bivouaced near STA.	8.10.
4.11.14	CASSELL	Marched via POPPERINGHE to YPRES. – camped at FARM N.W. of Pt 30 N. of B of BELLEWARDE F.H. 3.m. W. of YPRES arriving there about 8 p.m. (No.1 Camp)	Ref. Map B 10 1/40,000 Sheet 28
5.11.14	No.1. Camp	Horses + Transport sent to rare cover from view of aeroplanes. Camp shelled in afternoon. 3 men wounded. Regt. paraded dismounted 5 p.m. – took over trenches at 10 p.m. in HERONTHAGE WOOD facing W.	8.10.
6.11.14	TRENCHES. HERONTHAGE WOOD.	Severe outburst of rifle fire at 12 m.n. – two more 8 a.m. Severe outbursts of rifle fire at dawn + heavy shelling 9-10 a.m. – 12-2 p.m. Again heavy rifle fire stabbing. right of trenches was reinforced at 4 p.m. CAPTS. KEVIN-DAVIES. HODGEKINSON. LTS. TALBOT.	8.10.
7.11.14	ditto.	LAMBERT (1st R. Drs.) wounded. Heavy rifle fire 7 p.m. – 12 m.n. Relieved by 5th Fusiliers 2 a.m. arrived back at No.2 Camp 6.30 a.m. Total Casualties 57. 3 off: wounded 20 m.or. – men killed - 34 n.c.o's - men wounded	See Appendix I. [1]/A
		Marched 1 p.m. to FIELD N. of C. in CAMP 1 m.i. W. of YPRES (No.2 Camp.) Stood to " marched dismounted at 5 p.m.	2.10.
8.11.14	No. 2 Camp	to support LORD CAVAN'S BRIGADE + moved into camp near ZILLEBEKE. camp used: for horses so returned to No. 2. Camp. Turned out again 10 p.m. dismounted. but sent back to camp again	2.40.
9.11.14	No 2 Camp	Remained in No. 2. Camp. Major LOMER sent to hospital (CAPT. HODGKINSON reported died of wounds)	3.10.
		150 men of A.B.C. Sqdns. under Maj. MASON marched dismounted + occupied support trenches at ZILLEBEKE See Appendix II.	8.10.
10.11.14	No 2. Camp	at 7 p.m. + returned at daybreak. No casualties	
		Stood to 5.30 a.m. At 1 p.m. moved up dismounted in support of trench at ZILLEBEKE + moved up in evening into WOOD in rear of LORD CAVAN'S H.Q. to which was an LANE S.E. of E. in ZILLEBEKE, returned to No 2. Camp at 10 p.m. Lt. HORN. 1 man wounded by shrapnel in afternoon	2.40.

1247 W 3299 200,000 (E) 8/14 J.B.C. &A. Forms/C.2118/11.

Army Form C. 2118.

Page 2.

WAR DIARY
or
INTELLIGENCE SUMMARY

(Erase heading not required.)

Instructions regarding War Diaries and Intelligence Summaries are contained in F.S. Regs., Part II. and the Staff Manual respectively. Title pages will be prepared in manuscript.

Hour, Date, Place	Summary of Events and Information	Remarks and references to Appendices
11.11.14. No. 2 Camp.	Stood to 5:30 a.m. Exercise in inspection of horses + equipment, prepared to move at 12 noon, but orders for march's cancelled, moved up to support Lord Cavan at Zillebeke.	Ref Map BELGIUM Sheet 28. 2.V.O.
12.11.14. No. 2 Camp.	Marched early to Witte Poort F^m (No. 3 Camp) marched dismounted C squad in rear of Lord Cavan's No. at 1 p.m. in support of his infantry - at 5:30 p.m. moved into the trenches at ZILLEBEKE	2.V.O.
13.11.14. Trenches at ZILLEBEKE	Attack expected at 4:30 a.m. but there was very heavy shrapnel fire followed by rifle fire at 8:20 a.m. See Appendix III. Lt. Talbot reported killed at 9:30 a.m. - Maxim guns out of action. Relieved by Household Cav. returned to No. 3 Camp at 9 p.m. Casualties 6 killed 12 wounded. Total 18.	2.V.O.
14.11.14. No. 3 Camp.	Marched to Ben Broenen Jager (No. 4 Camp) 3 mi. S.W. of YPRES at 11:30 a.m. arriving 2 p.m. - bivouaced in Farm. Stood to for 3 hours.	2.V.O.
15.11.14. No. 4 Camp.	Marched to Station Sq. YPRES arriving 6 p.m. sent horses back to camp - took over trenches at 7:30 p.m. at ZILLEBEKE from Household Cav. Quiet night.	3.V.O.S. 2.V.O.
16.11.14. Trenches at ZILLEBEKE	A good deal of shelling all day induced to stay in trenches another 24 hrs. Spds. relieved one another from Supper trenches. 1 Sqdn. North Somerset Yeo. in centre trench, 2 Sqdns. N.S.Y. + one 3DG in support. Heavy rifle fire from 7:30 p.m. to 11:45 p.m. Afternoon was quiet.	2.V.O.
17.11.14. Trenches at ZILLEBEKE	Very heavy shelling all day from 9 a.m. R.S.M. Stewart killed 9:30 a.m. Cornwall mortally shelled kill 10:15 a.m. and 1:10 - 1 p.m. at which time "A" Sqdn. repulsed a heavy attack. A second heavy attack took place at 3:30 p.m. against "C" Sqdn. Capt. Wright 1/1st wounded then killed, Lt. Chapman killed Capt. Stewart wounded. N.C.O.s + men killed 14 Wounded 41 Total 55. Relieved by 2nd Life Guards.	See Appendix IV. 2.V.O.
18.11.14. No. 4 Camp.	Arrived No. 4 Camp 1:30 a.m. Led Horses were sent to meet Regt at Sta. Sq. YPRES (genuine meaning). Lt. Chapman reported as having died during the morning. Capt. Wright + Lt. Chapman buried at 11:30 a.m. in cemetery at YPRES. + R.S.M. Stewart at Mil. Hosp. YPRES. Congratulations from Gen Byng and 3rd Cav. Div. + Col. Campbell comdg. the brigade. - Lt. Gen Sir Douglas Haig. Snow fell	2.V.O.
19.11.14. No. 4 Camp.	Horse parade. re-adjusting of officers charges. Snow past.	2.V.O.
20.11.14. No. 4 Camp.	Billeting party + transport marched 7:15 a.m. for La Couronne 6 mi. S.W. of BAILLEUL. Regt marched with Brigade at 3 p.m. via QUEBRON, WESTOUTRE, METEREN, VIEUX BERQUIN, - arrived in billets at 3 a.m. in the L'EPINETTE CAUDESCURE district. Distance of march over 25 mi. roads very slippery with snow + past.	Ref Map FRANCE 1:80,000 SAINT-OMER. 2.V.O.

WAR DIARY or INTELLIGENCE SUMMARY

Army Form C. 2118.

Instructions regarding War Diaries and Intelligence Summaries are contained in F. S. Regs., Part II. and the Staff Manual respectively. Title pages will be prepared in manuscript.

(Erase heading not required.)

Page 3.

Hour, Date, Place	Summary of Events and Information	Remarks and references to Appendices
21.11.14. BILLETS L'EPINETTE, CAUDESCURE DISTRICT	Likely to remain in billets for some time. Commenced improving billets + horse accommodation. Training commenced. Weds. reserved for Brigade Scheme - Fris. for Regtl. Scheme. Training of Non-Machine Men &c. Res.	REF MAP. FRANCE 1:80,000 SAINT-OMER. 21B.
22.11.14. ditto	Lt. Dawson - 1st Reinforcements arrived 50 men - 46 horses.	D[itt]o.
29.11.14. ditto	Lt. Lyne with draft of 75 men - 60 horses arrived.	D[itt]o.
7.12.14. ditto	2nd Lt. Reeve from 16th Lancers (Coy) + Hon 2nd Lt. Greer from North Irish Horse (temp) joined.	D[itt]o.
8.12.14. ditto	Capt. Ponsonby A.S.D. Lts. Werthington Williams, Smith, Stewart, 19 men - 14 horses arrived	D[itt]o.
11.12.14. ditto	Inspection by Maj. Gen. Hon. J. Byrd, Cmdg. 3rd Cav Div.	D[itt]o.
13.12.14. ditto	Warned that Brigade would be required to move next day.	D[itt]o.
14.12.14. ditto	Marched 6 a.m. to BAILLEUL via BLEU - in to DRANOUTRE - ordered in reserve during an Infantry attack. Bivouacked that night in Fields S. end of BAILLEUL. but men in the large glasshouses of Ste VINERY.	D[itt]o. REF MAP. BELGIUM 1:100,000 OSTEND
15.12.14. BILLETS BAILLEUL	Stood to in the billets in reserve. At 10 pm Billeting parties marched to L'EPINETTE, CAUDESCURE	D[itt]o.
16.12.14. ditto		D[itt]o.
17.12.14. BILLETS L'EPINETTE, CAUDESCURE DISTRICT	Marched 9.30 am to former billets at L'EPINETTE, CAUDESCURE via BLEU arriving 12 noon.	REF MAP. FRANCE 1:80,000 SAINT-OMER.
20.12.14. ditto	Resumed to Training + improvement of Billets. Weather wet. Men - horses in good health. Football indulged in in spare hours.	D[itt]o.
25.12.14. ditto	Brigade stood to from 4pm - 11pm in case of being required to go to assistance of the Indian Div. near LA BASSÉE. Each Officer, N.C.O. Pte. rect. Xmas Card from Their Majesties THE KING and QUEEN and a gift from PRINCESS MARY, consisting of a decorated metal box containing packet of Tobacco + packet of Cigarettes, Xmas Card, also a pipe. Plum Puddings were provided by the A.S.C.	D[itt]o.
4.1.15. ditto	Inspection by Maj. Gen. E.H.H. Allenby, C. Cmdg. Cav. Corps.	D[itt]o.

3.D.4.

6th Cavalry Brigade

2nd
3. Dragoon Guards   121/4261

Vol III.   10 – 29.1.15

2nd DES

WAR DIARY
or
INTELLIGENCE SUMMARY

Army Form C. 2118.

PAGE 4

Hour, Date, Place	Summary of Events and Information	Remarks and references to Appendices
10.1.15 BILLETS L'EPINETTE (CAUDESCURE DISTRICT) 25.1.15	Major BURT joined also 1 NCO and 2 men. Learned that the Brigade would move on Jan 27th.	REF MAP FRANCE 1:80,000 SAINT OMER ERC
26.1.15 ditto	Billeting party went to area BLARINGHEM – STEINBECQUE	ditto ERC
27.1.15 "	Stood to at 7 AM. Inspection by F.M. SIR JOHN FRENCH at 2 PM.	ditto ERC
28.1.15 "	Regiment marched to new billets at BOESEGHEM arriving at 1:30 PM. Shooting at 10 AM.	ditto ERC
29.1.15 BILLETS BOESEGHEM	1 NCO and 2 PTES from RAMC joined.	ERC

M

121/44468

6th Cavalry Brigade

3rd Dragoon Guards.

Vol III. 2 — 25.2.15

Nil

WAR DIARY or INTELLIGENCE SUMMARY

Army Form C. 2118.

Page 5

Hour, Date, Place	Summary of Events and Information	Remarks and references to Appendices
2.2.15 BOESCHEPE	CAPT N MCLMORE and 2 billeting party proceeded to YPRES. CAPT LVOUSTON returned from sick leave in ENGLAND	REF MAP FRANCE / BELGIUM STANFORD
3.2.15 "	Regiment paraded at 3 PM at BOESCHEPE and rode to STEENVOORDE. Strength 250 rifles including officers (not including Machine Guns) & Staff. By motor omnibus from STEENVOORDE (3.30 PM) to YPRES (9 PM). Billeted N wall of the GRANDE PLACE.	ditto
4.2.15 YPRES	Orders to trenches issued. Battn shifted no casualties	REF MAP YPRES (TRENCHES) ditto (trenches square 22)
8.2.15 1 MILE SE OF ZILLEBEKE	Paraded YPRES GRANDE PLACE 10.30 PM and marched to trenches and took over from 3rd LIFE GUARDS (7th Cav Bde) A Sqdn on right, B Sqdn on left, C sqdn in support. NORTH SOMERSET YEOMANRY on right, 9th Lancers & 28th INF Bde on the left. Trenches guns with A Sqdn. Trenches muddy but weather fine and cold.	ditto
9.2.15 10.2.15 11.2.15 12.2.15	3 NCOs & 4 Ptes joined	
13.2.15	1 NCO wounded. Shelling but no shell fire. 2 Ptes wounded shell broaching the [illegible] trench [illegible] 3 Ptes killed by enemys trench mortar shell fired about 20 yards from 11 AM to 1 PM. Enemys trenches shelled by 2 British Batteries at 1 PM, and German trench mortar self [illegible] by [illegible] at 1 NCO and 1 Pte wounded, Batt'n very tired but own shelling about 2 PM. The Brigade was relieved at 9.30 PM by 4 B Cav Bde 6th Dragoon Guards relieving 2 RHG in trenches. After finding all arrangements [illegible] officers & NCOs required [illegible] & B sqdn guards left marched post + night with 2 & D sqdn	ditto 3 1 1 ditto 3 1 1 EACH

WAR DIARY or INTELLIGENCE SUMMARY

Army Form C. 2118.

page 6

Hour, Date, Place	Summary of Events and Information	Remarks and references to Appendices
13.2.15 (continued) YPRES	Enlisted into commission at 2 P.M. arrival at	REF MAP FRANCE 1:80000 STOMER ERC
21.2.15 BOESEGHEM	Orders came. Entrained of a rapid BOESEGHEM & form strength 300 officers 2 C.O.s and men and 1 machine gun	ditto STOMER ERC
23.2.15.	and 690 or moto horses at BOESEGHEM 1530 yards for men and 1000 average per machine gun carried 1 Officer and 33 men per Sqdn sent on the days to billets at FONTAINE HOUCK place later. The horses of 1st Cav Div were to be brushed. Machine gun section attached for duty with 1st Cav Divn at YPRES proceeds thither under the command of 2/Lt STEWART.	ditto ERC
25.2.15.	1st H.L.T. rejoined 2/Lt STEWART at YPRES.	ditto ERC

6th Cavalry Brigade

3rd Dragoon Guards.

Vol IV 2 – 31. 3. 15.

War diary. Bandyis.
3rd (Prince of Wales) Dragoon Guards

WAR DIARY
or
INTELLIGENCE SUMMARY
(Erase heading not required.)

Army Form C. 2118.

Hour, Date, Place	Summary of Events and Information	Remarks and references to Appendices
BOESEGHEM. MARCH 2nd	Draft of 14 O.R. arrived from the Base.	REF MAP. HAZEBROUCK SHEET 5A SHEET 5
" 9th	The regiment provided three Officers and sixty-seven N.C.O.'s and men to dig the reserve defensive line of trenches at STEENBECQUE.	
" 10th	Orders received that the Brigade would move the next day.	
" 11th	Paraded at 5.30 A.M. and marched to the Brigade rendezvous at STEENBECQUE, thence to the Divisional rendezvous at LAMOTTE au BOIS, halted there from 7.30 A.M until 3 P.M. billeted in MERVILLE. Men all under cover. Horses in the open.	
MERVILLE 12th	"Stood To" saddled up all day.	
" 13th	Afternoon returned to billets at BOESEGHEM.	
BOESEGHEM. " 14th	Capt. Hon REEVE STEVENSON left us, Lieut's ALLEN, KINGHAM and 2/Lieut's HORN and BLACK joined, replacing Capt. PARSONBY D.S.O. & Lieut REEVES.	
" 15th	Lyne and STEWART at the regiment went through k rounds of 1 hour Battle Drill of the Order to Sergeant Regimental in daywork.	
" 16th	After WORTHINGTON formed instructing the brigade Officers and 100 N.C.O.'s and men the important practice instructed Lieut KINGHAM for trench digging.	

Army Form C. 2118.

WAR DIARY
or
~~INTELLIGENCE~~ SUMMARY
(Erase heading not required.)

Instructions regarding War Diaries and Intelligence Summaries are contained in F. S. Regs., Part II. and the Staff Manual respectively. Title pages will be prepared in manuscript.

Hour, Date, Place	Summary of Events and Information	Remarks and references to Appendices
Page 1 / BOTSFONTEIN MARCH 22nd 25th 31st	Horse inspection by O.C. L.H. Both and DDVS. 2/Lieut J GREER transferred to Base Inspection by O.C. L.H. for L.S.H. Inspection of the regiment by Brigadier orders by Capt F.A.S. MOORE A.V.C. Transferred to Second Mass Corps, SALISBURY.	REF. MAP HARTEBEESTPOORT SHEET 3rd EAR

3rd Cavalry Division

3rd Dragoon Guards
Vol X 1 — 30.4.15

WAR DIARY
or
INTELLIGENCE SUMMARY

(Erase heading not required.)

Army Form C. 2118.

Instructions regarding War Diaries and Intelligence Summaries are contained in F. S. Regs, Part II. and the Staff Manual respectively. Title pages will be prepared in manuscript.

Hour, Date, Place	Summary of Events and Information	Remarks and references to Appendices
April 1st 1915	Regiment in Billets at BOESINGHAM.	
" 2nd "	" " "	
" 3. IV 1915	Billets at BOESINGHAM. Regimental Scheme.	
4th IV 1915	Squadron Routine.	
5 IV 1915	Regiment paraded for inspection by Sir Julian Byng. C.O left for England.	
6 IV 1915	Major Burt took over command for 10 days. Billets BOESINGHAM.	
7 IV 1915	Regimental Field Day.	
8 IV 1915	Regimental Scheme	
9 IV 1915	Regimental programme of work	
10 IV 1915	Squadron arrangements. Programme of work	
11 IV 1915	Billets BOESINGHAM.	
12 IV 1915	Night Scheme	
13 IV 1915	Billets BOESINGHAM.	
14 IV 1915	Regimental Programme of work carried out.	
15 IV 1915	Regimental Field day. Continued	
16 IV 1915	Billets at ROESINGHAM	
17 IV 1915	Billets Left H.Q. & posted to B Squadron	
18 IV 1915	Capt Bates left H.Q. & posted to B Squadron	
19 IV 1915	Billets BOESINGHAM Regimental Routine	
20 IV 1915	" "	
21 IV 1915	" "	
22 IV 1915	Regimental Field Day	
23 IV 1915	Orders received to stand to at breakfast at 11 A.M. Officers resumed to head up at Leave at 1.8s. Colonel Bingham B.S.O. was Brigadier. Regiment left BOESINGHAM 1.30 PM. Marched thro HAZEBROUCK to A BEELE & found the Cavalry Corps together Stayed in field at A BEELE at 9.30 PM. received orders to billet at EECKE	
24 IV 1915	Regiment moved at 8 AM. route MONT. DES. CATS, & place S of VLAMERTINGHE and remained there until 7 PM then went to billets at BOESCHEPE arriving 9 PM.	
25 IV 1915	Stood to 6AM moved 9am & point S of POPERING H.E. marched at 3 PM to a point N.W. of POPERINGNE. Shelling both heavy. Regt. left to the fields to the left at 4.30 PM & moved to HOUTKERQUE & Billeted there for the night.	

Army Form C. 2118.

WAR DIARY
or
INTELLIGENCE SUMMARY
(Erase heading not required.)

Instructions regarding War Diaries and Intelligence Summaries are contained in F.S. Regs., Part II. and the Staff Manual respectively. Title pages will be prepared in manuscript.

April

Hour, Date, Place	Summary of Events and Information	Remarks and references to Appendices
April 26th IV 1915	The Regiment started to at 6 P.M. Moved at 6.30 A.M. to FRONTIER BRIDGE; at Noon moved to a place just west of POPERINGHE, offsaddled and stayed there until 9.30 P.M. Moved to a place near POPERINGHE, left the horses in fields + marched on through it, arriving at POPERINGHE. The enemy shelled the town. No shells dropped near the Regiment.	
April 27th IV 1915	The march was continued. H.Q. marched to VLAMERTINGHE and billeted near the station, arriving at 2.30 A.M. Shelling commenced in POPERINGHE about 4 P.M. The Regiment moved to a field. Later moved to a farm 800 X S.W. of VLAMERTINGHE at 8 P.M. Received orders to go to the Trenches, but order was cancelled at 9 P.M. Received orders to Stand to on horses. At 12 noon marched to FORGE, arrived there + Billeted at 8.30 P.M.	
April 28th 1915	Moved at 8 A.M. to POPERINGHE. Remained there + returned to Billets at 6.30 P.M.	
April 29th 1915	Stayed in Billets.	
April 30th 1915	Moved to POPERINGHE about noon + returned to Billets at dusk.	

6/3

157/5gu

3rd Cavalry Division

2nd Dragoon Guards &

Vol VI 1 — 30. 5.15

Army Form C. 2118.

WAR DIARY
or
INTELLIGENCE SUMMARY

(Erase heading not required.)

Instructions regarding War Diaries and Intelligence Summaries are contained in F. S. Regs., Part II. and the Staff Manual respectively. Title pages will be prepared in manuscript.

Hour, Date, Place	Summary of Events and Information	Remarks and references to Appendices
May 1st 1915.	AT VLAMERTINGHE. Marched to POPERINGHE	
2nd	Left POPERINGHE & returned to Billets	
3rd	BOESINGHEM. Billets.	
4th	Billets at BOESINGHEM	
5th	Billets.	
6th		
7th	Marching to.	
8th		

WAR DIARY
or
INTELLIGENCE SUMMARY

(Erase heading not required.)

Army Form C. 2118.

Instructions regarding War Diaries and Intelligence Summaries are contained in F.S. Regs., Part II. and the Staff Manual respectively. Title pages will be prepared in manuscript.

Hour, Date, Place	Summary of Events and Information	Remarks and references to Appendices
May. 9. V.15. BOESEGHEM	The Regiment paraded at Renescure on the STEENBECKE Road at 1.P.M. + proceeded in Motor Buses. Strength including Officers 300 Officers Col. O.T.B. BINGHAM. D.S.O. Capt. TRACKER - NEVILLE. Col OWSTON Capt. COLES. Capt. BREYNARD. Lieuts. WORTHINGTON. GRIMSHAW Lt BENTON, NEWTON-DEAKIN, VINCENT, C.T.SMITH 2/Lt BEDFORD.	
May 10th V.15.	Stayed in Huts & dug out shelters near BRIELIN	
11.V.15	Party sent up to inspect Trenches near HOOGE being Lt WORTHINGTON. Lt NEWTON-DEAKIN. Lt VINCENT + C.T.SMITH	See appendix & reports from A, B & C Squadrons
12.V.15	The Regiment marched at 8.A.M. (Party in advance) & later over trenches from SHROPSHIRES, ARGYLE + SUTHERLAND, N.H. and IRISH FUSILIERS. Captain OWSTON was wounded in the Thigh at the Level-Crossing at RAILWAY WOOD. The Trenches were taken over about 11 P.M. Capt. COLES reported killed by rifle bullet in abdomen while going round his Squadron Trenches about 11.30 P.M. & 12 o'clock midnight	
13.V.15	A very heavy bombardment started at daylight & the final attack was made at 7.A.M. "A" Squadron on right with "C" on left as shown by map. "B" Centre "C" on right. The Troops Lt on left of "A" Squadron retired & enfiladed the trench. About 3.P.M. Capt. NEVILLE was shot through the head from the rear, & did not recover consciousness & died at dark. At midnight 13/14 May the IRISH FUSILIERS started to relieve us	Map (Sketch with report)

Army Form C. 2118.

WAR DIARY
or
INTELLIGENCE SUMMARY
(Erase heading not required.)

Hour, Date, Place	Summary of Events and Information	Remarks and references to Appendices
14.V.15.	The casualties during the fighting 12/13/14 May 1914 are as follows:- Killed. 12th Capt. COLES. Wounded Capt. OWSTON. Killed 13th Capt. TRACKER-NEVILLE. Wounded 12th Colonel O. B. BINGHAM. D.S.O " Captain. LESLIE " Lt. GRIMSHAW " Lt. C.T. SMITH (Since died of wounds) Total casualties during the operations .. 2 officers killed 5 wounded 28 men killed 40 wounded & missing. Total all ranks killed & wounded 79.	NB Lt Smith died of wounds
15 May. 1915	The Regt returned to VLAMERTINGHE. reinforcement arrived 2 Y.S.O. & 10 men	
16th " "	Rested at VLAMERTINGHE	
17 " "	Remained " "	
18 " "	" " "	
19 " "	" " "	
20 " "	" " "	
21st " "	The Regiment returned to BILLETS at BOESINGHAM.	

WAR DIARY
or
INTELLIGENCE SUMMARY
(Erase heading not required.)

Army Form C. 2118

May

Hour, Date, Place	Summary of Events and Information	Remarks and references to Appendices
20.5.15. BOESEGHEM	The Regiment returned to Billets at midday & under the Command of Major A. BURT at midnight. Sigld. Officers arrived Captain [P.D. STEWART] 2/Lt [A.C.M. FINLAY] 2/Lt [A.M. SAVAGE] 2/Lt [A.C. CLIFFORD] 2/Lt [G.P.R. ALLSOP] 2/Lt [E.S.B. RHODES] 2Lt [HEAD] 2Lt [W.B. HATHORN] Also a draft of 30 men from Canterbury & 10 from Rouen.	app. no. 7
21.V.15 BOESEGHEM	In Billets. Regiment refitting.	app. no. 7
22.V.15 " "	In Billets. Regiment refitting	app. no. 7
23.V.15 " "	Sunday. Refitting	app. no. 7
24.V.15 " "	In Billets. Half field day scheme by Major Burt returns to Billets 2:30 PM	app. no. 7
25.V.15 " "	In Billets. Squadron Drill, under Squadron arrangements	app. no. 7
26.V.15 " "	In Billets. 13 Horses arrived Late (R.J.)	app. no. 7
27.V.15 " "	In Billets. Horse paid to Squadron	app. no. 7
28.V.15 " "	In Billets. 3 officers went to T. Worthington 2Lt [Hathorn] Lt [HOLROYD-SMITH]	
29.V.15 "	To Coffee men Trenches, and the Regiment left about 1PM in Busses Officers Major BURT Major Mason Capt P.D. STEWART. Lt HOLT Lt HORNE Lt ALLEN. 2Lt SAVAGE 2Lt BLACK. 2Lt DADSON & Capt. KEVILL-DAVIS.	
30 V. 15	In the Trenches near HOOGE. S. of MENIN ROAD. B. Squadron Left. A sqdn Centre. C. Right with Royals on C's right. The night passed fairly quietly. A lot of sniping. Major Burt commands left End. Sector. Heavy Shelling started from high & heavy shells. Capt. P.D. Stewart Lt Dadson Black all wounded. Capt. KEVILL DAVIS was wounded going up to the trenches. L/Cpl [BENTON & FINLAY 2Lt VINCENT & SAVAGE] arrived as reinforcements & went to the trenches	

3rd Cavalry Division

3rd Dragoon Guards.
Part of Vol VII   31.5.15 —— 5.6.15

12/9/49

WAR DIARY
or
INTELLIGENCE SUMMARY
(Erase heading not required.)

Army Form C. 2118.

Instructions regarding War Diaries and Intelligence Summaries are contained in F.S. Regs, Part II. and the Staff Manual respectively. Title pages will be prepared in manuscript.

Hour, Date, Place	Summary of Events and Information	Remarks and references to Appendices
31st May.	Fairly quiet. "C" Sqn dug a new trench. Between 'C' & 'A' Sqn in centre of 'C' Sqn. The trenches were completely enfiladed, communication was kept up by men lying in the open. At dusk Lieut. Katenkio occupied the stables of the CHATEAU. No opposition offered. The CHATEAU was heavily shelled at 7 a.m. and the party fell back on the stable where a post remained until 3 p.m. The Germans shelled our trenches. CHATEAU and HOOGE from 10.30 a.m. until 12 noon, and from 2 p.m. to 4 p.m. Casualties 4 killed - 9 wounded.	
1st June.	Trenches shelled from 11 a.m - 12.30 p.m. recommenced 2.30 p.m. and finished 6 p.m. Casualties 9 killed, 14 wounded. No attack was made.	
2nd June.	At 6 a.m. our trenches were shelled with high explosive until 12 noon. During the lull all blown in trenches were rebuilt as much as possible. 2/Lt. A.C. Clifford was killed by a shell while lifting his Maxim gun over the parapet, in order to assist in repelling an attack. This attack was beaten off. The Germans recommenced to shell our trenches. All 'C' Sqn trenches, a portion of 'A' Sqn. and the communication trenches were blown in. The supports were heavily shelled at this time. At 3.30 p.m. a party of Germans moved up towards the junction of 3.D.Gds and 1st Royals. A machine gun of the Royals	

WAR DIARY
or
INTELLIGENCE SUMMARY
(Erase heading not required.)

Army Form C. 2118.

Hour, Date, Place	Summary of Events and Information	Remarks and references to Appendices
	Turned on the Germans and stopped them. At dusk the trenches were fully occupied and relit. Heavy sniping all night. <u>Casualties</u>	
	1 Officer killed - 2/Lt A.C. Clifford. 10 Other men killed 30 " wounded 4 " missing (since accounted for).	
3rd June.	Relieved by 1st Lincolns at 1.30 a.m. Royal Fusiliers relieved K.D.G's. The Regiment went in reserve to Ramparts at YPRES. Casualties - Killed 1. Wounded 4.	
4th June.	Still in reserve at YPRES. Marched back to VLAMERTINGHE.	
5th June.	In reserve at VLAMERTINGHE.	

151/59/4

3rd Cavalry Division

8th Dragoon Guards

Vol VII   31.5 —— 30.6.15

WAR DIARY or INTELLIGENCE SUMMARY

Army Form C. 2118

Hour, Date, Place	Summary of Events and Information	Remarks and references to Appendices
31st V. 15	Sniping continued all day & some heavy shell fire. The Chateau of HOOGE was alleged occupied by "B" Sqdn on the left of B.M. of Menin Road was in K.D. 9th Shelling pretty heavy. Casualties 8 men killed, 12 wounded, right badly hurt.	
1st June VI. 15	Shelling commenced with high explosive about 8 mm. ceased about 12 noon & commenced about 1.25 & went on til 2 P.M. Trenches were rebuilt but "C" Sqdn trench was very badly to wit & the spare & kept firing on it. Burton tks. on left. 1 Off. + 2 L/c. Finlay. 3 o.r. & 4 or. thus on N.S.W. Casualties 2 killed, 8 wounded	
2nd VI. 15	Very heavy shelling at 4 A.M. & lasted continuously until 12 noon nearly all the trenches were completely blown in during the lull from noon to 1.25 P.M. the Trenches were rebuilt as well as possible. The shelling was very severe & all the communication trenches heavily shelled & were destroyed the support & reserve trenches heavily shelled & The Dragoons ground Lt Clifford even killed about 3 P.M. The Surrey made several fine heroic attacks but were driven back. 1st M.G. on the left with "B" Sqdn. doing good work. Total Casualties for June 2nd 1 Officer killed & 19 men & 38 men wounded. Gun returned by the 1st Dragoons about 1.00 A.M. & the Sqdn. relief to the Ramparts at Ypres in reserve. Casualties 1 man killed 2 wounded Lt FINLAY	
3rd June VI. 15	In reserve at Ramparts at Ypres all men very worn	
4th VI. 15	Went to VLAMERTINGHE & saw 15 the Burial of Lt A.C. CLIFFORD in the Reserve near the Church.	
5th VI. 15	Heavy shelling took place at Ypres & gun bombs and one casualty. 1 killed 4 wounded. Regiment arrived about 11 P.M. at VLAMERTINGHE & Bivouacked in field near Solution "A"	
6 V. 15	L/t Harris Sykes Hellyer LONGBOTHAM joined 2nd Regiment at Scheme under September at G.O.C.	

WAR DIARY
or
INTELLIGENCE SUMMARY
(Erase heading not required.)

Army Form C. 2118.

Instructions regarding War Diaries and Intelligence Summaries are contained in F. S. Regs., Part II. and the Staff Manual respectively. Title pages will be prepared in manuscript.

Hour, Date, Place	Summary of Events and Information	Remarks and references to Appendices
June 7th 1915.	Returned to Billets at BOESINGHAM.	
8	Resting & refitting 5 O.R. joined from ROUEN.	
9	Billets at BOESINGHAM. Inspection by A.D.V.S. of Horses.	
10	" "	
11	" "	
12	Draft arrived 1 Sgt. & 44 other ranks. LT A J JOHNSON joined	
13	LT A.Q.M. FINLAY assumed HS duties of Adjutant	
14, 15	BILLETS	
16, 17, 18		
19	Draft arrived from England, 1 S.M. 1 Sgt. & 87 O.R. Regimental Marching	
20	order parade	
21	Squadron arrangements	
22	BOESINGHAM. Billets.	
23	Regiment was inspected by General Kenal.	
24	Marching order parade inspection by G.O.C.	
25	Squadron arrangements	
26	do	
27	2 LT. BEDFORD Joined ff strength N.O. Witham.	
28	Regimental rehearse under G.O.C.	
29	LT BENTON & 66 O.R. went in a digging party to a place near NRHUITIERS.	
30	Regimental Scheme under supervision of G.O.C.	

181/6/49

3rd Cavalry Division

3rd Dragoon Guards

Vol VIII   1 — 31.7.15.

WAR DIARY
or
INTELLIGENCE SUMMARY

(Erase heading not required.)

Army Form C. 2118

Instructions regarding War Diaries and Intelligence Summaries are contained in F.S. Regs., Part II. and the Staff Manual respectively. Title pages will be prepared in manuscript.

Hour, Date, Place	Summary of Events and Information	Remarks and references to Appendices
July 1st 1915.	Regimental Scheme, under the supervision of the S.O.C. crossing the Canal at NIEPPE. Swimming the horses.	
2nd	Sqdn. Arrangements.	
3rd – 5th	Sqdn. Arrangements.	
6th	2/Lt. E.S.D. Alsop & 6 other ranks marched to NIEUVE EGLISE to relieve party that went up different on 29th June 1915.	
7th	Regtl. scheme made including from S.O.C. 6 Cav. Bde.	
8th	Sqdn. Arrangements.	
9th – 10th	" "	
11th	A draft of 6 other ranks joined from Rouen.	
	2/Lt. W.B. Hatton & 94 other ranks proceeded to SAILLY sur la LYS for Trench digging.	
12th	Practice in canal crossing under service conditions.	
13 – 17th	Sqdn. Arrangements.	
18th	Regiment kept at SAILLY sur la LYS rejoined regt.	
19th	Regimental scheme. LE HOCQUET – WITTES RIDGE.	
20th	D: Squ. duty at NEUVE EGLISE relieved by party of same strength. 2/Lt. S.B. Flewin in charge 2/Lt. L. Hilyer	

WAR DIARY
or
INTELLIGENCE SUMMARY
(Erase heading not required.)

Army Form C. 2118.

Hour, Date, Place	Summary of Events and Information	Remarks and references to Appendices
21st	Work parties up & handed over. Capt. J.H. Hayes & 7th C.R. Stratham and a party of 59 other ranks detailed for digging at ELVERDINGHE	
22nd		
23rd		
24th	Capt. L.V. Owen rejoined from sick leave.	
25th	Lieutenant Crampton	
26th	NEUVE EGLISE digging party with exception of 18 other ranks rejoined	
	Similar arrangements	
	Regt. about 300 strong paraded at 2 p.m. for burial	
	digging at ELVERDINGHE. Capt. Hayes & party to remain	
	there. Lt. Col. A. Burt in command.	
27th		
28th	Regt. turned out 8 p.m. Lieuts. B's & others —	
29th	2Lt/Lt. O.B.S. Smith-Bingham & S.O. rejoined from overseas.	
30th		
31st	12 other ranks Lewis Machine Gunners joined from ROUEN	

12/6737

VIII

3rd Cavalry Division

3rd Dragoon Guards
Vol IX
August 15

Army Form C. 2118

WAR DIARY
or
INTELLIGENCE SUMMARY
(Erase heading not required.)

Instructions regarding War Diaries and Intelligence Summaries are contained in F.S. Regs., Part II. and the Staff Manual respectively. Title pages will be prepared in manuscript.

Hour, Date, Place	Summary of Events and Information	Remarks and references to Appendices
August 1st	Capt. L.V. Owston & Lt. J. Donald returned to billets from ELVERDINGHE. Regiment digging. Echelon B in billets.	M.S.R.
August 2nd		M.S.R.
August 3rd	Col. Bingham & Major Mason visited new billeting area.	M.S.R.
August 4th	A Regimental billeting party composed of Col. Bingham, Capt. Owston, Major Mason, Capt. Worthington, Lieut. Johnson & 2/Lt. Sykes & R.S.M.s & Intelligence proceeded to new billeting area to select billets. The billets selected were as follows:— 'A' Sqn. at WITTERNESSE. 'B' Sqn. & Regt. H.Q. at LIETTRES. 'C' Sqn. at QUERNES.	M.S.R.
August 5th	Capt. Owston went to new billeting area and selected LINGHEM as Regtl. H.Q. Regimental digging party returned to BOESEGHEM from ELVERDINGHE at 9.30 p.m.	M.S.R.
August 6th	Echelon 'B' under R.Q.M.S. Hannant paraded at the cross roads S. of the Inn E in BOESEGHEM at 9.45 a.m. previous to proceeding to new billets. The Regiment & Echelon A paraded at the same place in echelon B at 10.15 a.m. The Squadrons & moved off to new billets at 10.45 a.m. were in their billets by 1 p.m.	Reference Sheet 5a. Hazebrouck map 1/4. Reference attached map.

WAR DIARY
or
INTELLIGENCE SUMMARY
(Erase heading not required.)

Army Form C. 2118.

Hour, Date, Place	Summary of Events and Information	Remarks and references to Appendices
August 7th & 8th	Regiment in billets. Draft of 2 O.R. & 2 horses arrived on 8th from ROUEN.	W.D.R.
August 9th – 11th August 12th	Special arrangements. Marching out inspection of A & B & C Sqdns. by Commanding Officer. Capt. Austin transferred from H.Q. to C Sqdn. Lieut. Kelly transferred from "M.G. to H.Q." as adjutant. Lieut. A.C.M. Finlay rejoined from sick leave.	W.D.R. W.D.R.
August 13th	Marching out inspection of M.G. & H.Q. by Inspector of cavalry Commanding Officer. D.A.D.O.S. Rigging party, consisting of Major Lieut. Capt. Austin, Capt. Watherston, Lieut. Benton, Lieut. Katinskie, Lieut. Finlay, Lieut. Rhodes & 200 Other ranks proceeded in motor buses to ARMENTIÈRES.	W.D.R.
August 14th	Draft of 3 O.R. & 6 horses joined from Rouen.	W.D.R.
August 15th	2/Lieut. Vincent rejoined from sick leave.	W.D.R.
August 16th – 18th August 20th	Billets. Colonel Pierce arrived from England. Lt Katinskie admitted sick to hospital from ARMENTIÈRES.	W.D.R.

Army Form C. 2118

WAR DIARY
or
INTELLIGENCE SUMMARY

(Erase heading not required.)

Instructions regarding War Diaries and Intelligence Summaries are contained in F. S. Regs., Part II. and the Staff Manual respectively. Title pages will be prepared in manuscript.

Hour, Date, Place	Summary of Events and Information	Remarks and references to Appendices
August 21st	Col. Mercer left Regiment to be attached to 12th Division for 2 days experience of trench warfare. 3 O.R. + 2 horses returned from ROUEN.	W.S.R.
August 22nd — 26th	Billets.	
August 27th	Draft of 3 O.R. + 3 horses arrived from ROUEN	W.S.R.
August 28th	Draft of 20 N.C.Os + men left billets en route for LENIEPPE for work cutting in BOIS DE NIEPPE	W.S.R.
	Re wood cutting in BOIS DE NIEPPE	W.S.R.
August 29th	Pte. PINKNEY (M.G. Section) killed by shell at ARMENTIÈRES	W.S.R.
August 30th	Lieut. Findlay returned to billets from ARMENTIÈRES	W.S.R.
August 31st	French funder per cadres to ROUEN surplus R. establishment.	

1247 W 3299 200,000 (E) 8/14 J.B.C. & A. Forms/C. 2118/11.

Billeting Area.
6th Cav Bde.

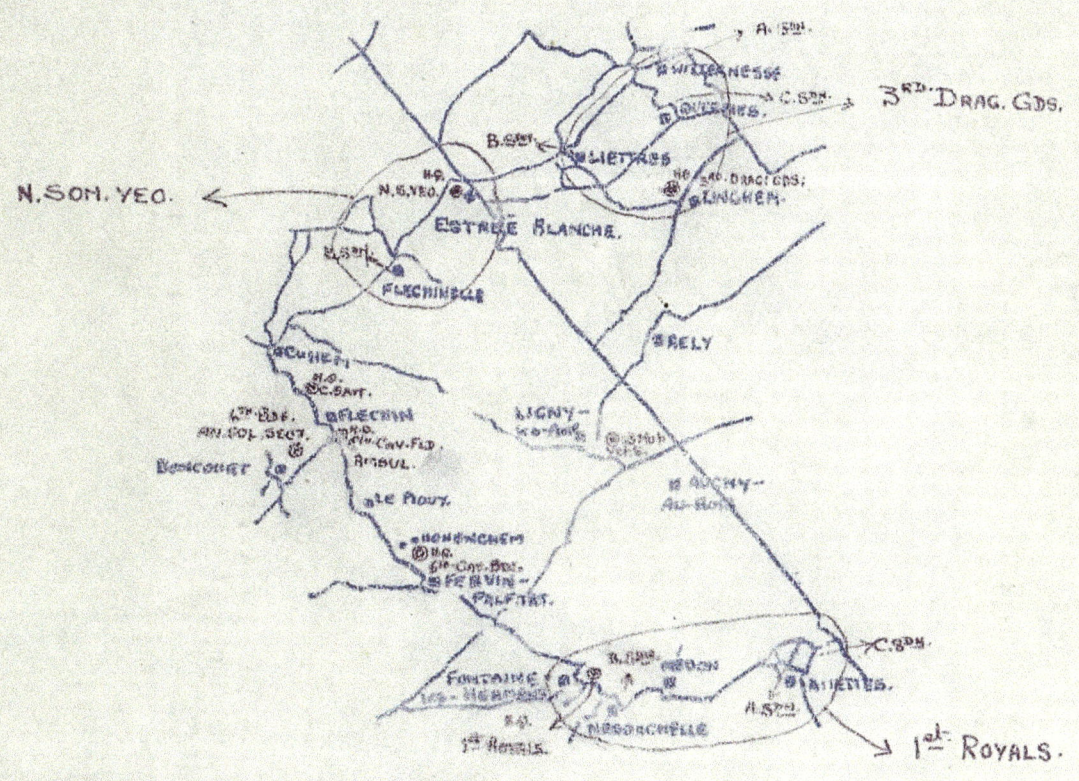

Scale: One inch to 1·58 mile.

6th Cav.Bde.
3rd Cav.Div.

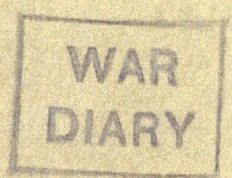

3rd DRAGOON GUARDS.

SEPTEMBER AND OCTOBER

1915

Hour, Date, Place	Summary of Events and Information	Remarks and references to Appendices
1st September	Billets	
2nd "	'B' Sqn. commenced squadron training. Sgt Trumpeter Swallow joined from ROUEN.	
3rd "		
4th "	Draft of 17 O.R. & 7 horses arrived from ROUEN.	
5th & 6th "	Riding party returned to billets from ARMENTIÈRES.	
7th "	'A' & 'C' Sqns. commenced squadron training.	
8th "	Sqn. training continued. Inspection of equipment by D.A.D.O.S.	
9th "	Sqn. training.	
	1 Section per troop of each squadron & all officers proceeded to Brigade H.Q. to witness the difference of smoke schemes & gas mask chlorine gas. Farrier Sgt. M⁽ᶜ⁾Shan joined from ROUEN.	
10th "	Brigade scheme carried out in area Bethune THEROUANNE and B.M.Y. under the Brigadier.	
11th "	Scheme carried out between 1st & 6th Brigades in FLECHIN area. 7 horses arrived from ROUEN.	
12th "	Billets.	
13th "	Billets.	
14th "	Inspection of Echelon 'A' complete - by G.O.C. 1st Bde.	
15th "	Billets - Joining horses joined from ROUEN.	

(Erase heading not required.)

Hour, Date, Place	Summary of Events and Information	Remarks and references to Appendices
16th Sept.	Billets.	
17th "	Regtl. Scheme.	
18th "	Regt. N.2 move this billets from LINGHEM to WITTERNESSE. Draft of 5 NCO's 5 men and 29 riding horses joined from ROUEN.	
19th "	Billets.	
20th "	Secret orders were received that the Bde. was going to move. Squadron marching orders forwarded were ordered for this day. At 6 p.m. the Regiment rendezvoused at the LINGHEM – LATIRMAND – LIETTRES – LA COUTURE – RELY cross roads. Order of march 'B','C','A', M.G., Echelon 'A' in rear of Regiments. Echelon 'B' Transport concentrated in the Chateau grounds LIETTRES. The regiment marched to the Bde. rendezvous at BELLERY. The brigade then marched to the BOIS DES DAMES, via FERFAY, MARLES LES MINES, where it arrived about 12 midnight, & went into bivouac for the night.	See Appendix.
21st "	Still in BOIS DES DAMES. Captain Austin, 1 N.C.O. 4 men transferred to 3 C.D. ammunt. Car Section.	
22nd "	" " "	
23rd "	" " "	
24th "	" " "	
25th "	" " " under short notice to move.	
26th "	Early reveille. Moved off at 5.30 a.m. when the Bde. marched to NOUEX-LES-MINES, thence to VERMELLES where the Regt. bivouacked for the night.	
27th "	VERMELLES. At 12.30 p.m. the Bde. were ordered to proceed dismounted to take up a position near LOOS. Yunches at LOOS.	

(Erase heading not required.)

Hour, Date, Place	Summary of Events and Information	Remarks and references to Appendices
28th Sept.	En route to LOOS. On sight of A.G. orders Wilson joined Echelon 'B' from ROUEN.	
	At LOOS. Regiment was relieved by Sussex Regt. at about 12 midnight. Squadrons marched independently to horses which were in bivouac at/near NOYELLE LES VERMELLES, arriving about 3 a.m. 29th.	
29th	11-30 a.m. the Regt. was ordered to march to BOIS DES DAMES where it went into bivouac. The weather was bad, being cold and wet.	
30th	Still in bivouac.	
1st Oct.	"	
2nd	"	
3rd	Regt. ordered to hold themselves in readiness to move. A billeting party was sent out under Capt. Worthington, Lt. Nevill-Deakin & H.Q. r. Sqn. Interpreter.	
	At 11 a.m. the Regiment received orders to be formed up ready to move at 12-30 p.m., but owing to a Division of the Infantry marching along part of the route selected, the Brigade was delayed and did not move off until about 3 p.m. The Regt. arrived at RAIMBERT about 5 p.m. & was billeted in the various nurse buildings.	
4th	In billets — Squadron arrangements.	
5th	2/Lieuts. W. Black and T. Kohler joined from Canterbury.	
6th	A bomb throwing party commenced training under 2/Lieut. T. Kohler. The party was composed of 3 N.C.Os and 27 men.	

Hour, Date, Place	Summary of Events and Information	Remarks and references to Appendices
7th October	Bombers training. Squadron exercise. 2/Lieuts M.J. Clery and B.H. Doncaster joined from Canterbury.	
8th & 9th "	Billets. Squadron arrangements.	
10th "	Draft of 9 N.C.Os and 41 men, 39 riding horses joined from ROUEN.	
11th "	Bombers carried on training.	
12th "	"	
13th "	Sqdn. Leaders met C.O. at Regt. Hd. Qrs. at 12 noon, when they went over the ground where it was proposed to carry out a scheme.	
14th "	Regt. Trench counter attack scheme.	
15th & 16th "	Billets. Sqdn. arrangements.	
17th "	Draft of 8 men joined from ROUEN.	
18th "	Received orders to move billets next day.	
19th "	Regt. marched from RAIMBERT to BEAUMETZ-LEZ-AIRE, where it stayed for the night. 2/Lieut. Johnson admitted to hospital.	
20th "	Still in billets.	
21st "	Regt. ordered to parade at 10-15 a.m. & marched into winter billets. The Regt. arrived in its billeting area about 12-15 p.m., when squadrons occupied billets as follows:- "A" Sqdn. at WESTREHEM, "B" Sqdn. FONTAINE-LEZ-HERMANS, "C" Sqdn. Hd. Qrs. & M.G. Section at NEDONCHELLE. A dismounted squadron of 2 officers & 100 N.C.Os & men joined from Base. 2/Lieut. Black admitted to hospital.	
22nd "	Regt. cleaned up billets and stables.	

(Erase heading not required.)

Hour, Date, Place	Summary of Events and Information	Remarks and references to Appendices
23rd Oct/15	Sqdn. arrangements.	
24th "	"M.G." Section left their billets in NEDONCHELLE and took up post ones in NEDON.	
25th "	Sqdns. commenced to build horse shelters.	
26th "	Billets.	
27th "	6, o.R, A.S.C. 12 heavy draught and 3 B.S. Ry wagons joined.	
28th "	Billets.	
29th "	2/Lieut. M.H. Dobson, 3 other ranks and 4 riding horses joined from ROUEN.	
30th "	2/Lieut. Johnson struck off strength of Regiment. 2/Lieut. Black rejoined regiment from hospital. 2/Lieut. S.B. Horn promoted Lieut. from 27-9-15. Lieut. R.B. Allen appointed Adjutant from 18-9-15.	
31st "	Regt. still improving billets and horse shelters.	

Army Form C. 2118.

Nov + Dec
1915.

3 Offrs

WAR DIARY
or
INTELLIGENCE SUMMARY

(Erase heading not required.)

Instructions regarding War Diaries and Intelligence Summaries are contained in F.S. Regs., Part II. and the Staff Manual respectively. Title pages will be prepared in manuscript.

Hour, Date, Place	Summary of Events and Information	Remarks and references to Appendices
1st November /15.	Capt. Kingham 2/Lt. Rhodes. 6 N.C.O's & 32 men proceed to SERCUS for digging.	
2nd November	Billets	
3" "	2/Lt. Ismalin, & 4 N.C.O's & 76 men proceeded to SERCUS to join the previous digging party.	
4" "	A.D.V.S. inspected horses of regiment. Capt. P.D. Stewart rejoins from England.	
5" "	Billets.	
6" "	2/Lt. Osmaston, 3 NCO's, 167 men proceed to SERCUS to join the previous & parties digging. Regimental staff rode, conducted in Chinese kent, for Sqdn leaders & Serjts. Serjt. for Sqdn leaders & Serjts seconds in command.	
7" "	S.O.R. joins from ROUEN.	
8" "	Billets.	
9" "	Capt. Kingham, 2/Lt. Langstham, & 2 nd/Lt. Osmaston. with 6 NCO's & 150 men proceed by bus to OUDERDOM for trench digging.	
10" "	A.D.V.S. inspection of horses of regiment. Captain L.V. Owen seconded for service with M.M.G. Sec.	
11" + 12"	Billets	
13" - 16" "	Billets.	
17" "	Regt. paraded at 9 am. at FONTAINE-LES-HERMANS - arriving at OFFIN at 5:30 pm. & went into front billets. 'C' & 'A' Sqdns at LOISON. 'B' HQ+ M.G. at OFFIN.	
18" - 21st "	Training new billets. Musis Inspection of regiment on 21st. On 20th 1 NCO + 2 men + 2 riding horses joined from ROUEN.	
22nd	Billets.	

WAR DIARY or **INTELLIGENCE SUMMARY**

Army Form C. 2118.

3 Sqdn

Hour, Date, Place	Summary of Events and Information	Remarks and references to Appendices
23rd Nov. 15	Col. Burt in charge of 3rd Can Div. digging parties proceeded with Capt. Holroyd Smyth. 2/Lts Sykes - Bowdle & Sullivan + 183 O.R. to OUDERDOM.	
24th - 26th	Ditto	
26th	2/Lts. Clery & Keller attached to 46th Inf Bde for instruction to the 1st Dec.	
27th	2/Lt Osmaston & Rhodes attached to 46th Inf Bde for instruction to the 1st Dec.	
28 & 29th	2 O.R. 7 men 1 L.D. joined from ROUEN	
30th	Billets	
Dec 1st	All Markets in regiment anaesthetised. Digging party returned from OUDERDOM.	
2nd	Got new clothing disinfected.	
3rd	Lt. H.A. Grimshaw, 2/Lt M. Nutt and G.A. Whittell joined from Canterbury.	
4th	New clothing disinfected.	
5th	1 O.R. & 3 R. Horses joined from the Base.	
6th	18 O.R. joined from Base.	
7th	Horse inspection by A.D.V.S. at OFFIN.	
	A dismounted marching order parade was held at OFFIN of the 3 D.G. Corp formed in accordance with recent orders issued previously.	
8th	Musical inspection of parts.	
9th	Transport for digging party, Capt Tillett, attached, 1 N.C.O 6 drivers 13 horses 3 wagons proceed to LA BELLE HOTESSE for digging purpose.	
10th	Digging party for LA BELLE HOTESSE proceeded today, strength 2 officers (Capt. Worthington, 2/Lt Rhodes, 2/Lt. Slade) 86 rank + file.	
11th	8 O.R. 13 return & 1 R. draught horses joined from Base.	
12th	Billets	

Army Form C. 2118.

WAR DIARY
or
INTELLIGENCE SUMMARY
(Erase heading not required.)

3 D Coy

Hour, Date, Place	Summary of Events and Information	Remarks and references to Appendices
Dec. 13th	A 2nd party proceeded to LA BELLE HOTESSE for digging. 1 Officer (2/Lt. Harris) 92 rank & file. All wheeled transport of regt. was inspected at LOISON by O.C. A.S.C. 3rd D.	
" 14th–18th	Billets.	
" 19th	A.D.V.S. commenced carrying out the mallein test.	
" 20–21st	Test continued. Billets.	
" 22nd	H.Q. & M.G. were medically inspected.	
" 23rd	B Sqdn. medically inspected.	
" 24th	The two digging parties from LA BELLE HOTESSE returned to billets.	
" 26th	Xmas day. 3 O.R. and 1 R. horse joined from base.	
" 26th–27th	Billets. 2/Lt. H.Q. and dismounted Coy. paraded at OFFIN. Orders received to furnish H.Q. of the dismounted battalion found by the Brigade.	
" 28th	B m'td. Coy. and H.Q. went for route march.	
" 29th	Training of dismtd. Coy. continued.	
" 30th/31st	3/Lt. 2 O.R. joined from ROUEN. 2/Lt. Alsop to hospital.	

WAR DIARY

3RD (P of W's) DRAGOON GDS

PERIOD:- FROM 1-1-16 TO 27-3-16

Vol IX, X & XI

January, February, March 1916.

WAR DIARY or INTELLIGENCE SUMMARY

Army Form C. 2118.

3rd Dragoon Guards

Title pages: Jan. Front 1915

Place	Date	Hour	Summary of Events and Information	Remarks and references to Appendices
	Jan. 1 5/1/16	1 a.m. 2 a.m. 3 a.m. 4 a.m.	M.G. detachment, Lieut. H.P. Holt, & Lieut. S.B. Horn + 40 O.R. proceeded to BETHUNE by road. Dismtd. Coy. parade. Transport entrained for dismtd. Coy. and proceeded to BETHUNE. Transport by rail. Battn. H.Q. + 2 platoons of dismtd. cos. (mostly 'B' Sqdn. paraded at OFFIN at 5.30 a.m. Platoons from 'A' + 'C' Sqdn. joined the column at LOISON. The Coy. and H.Q. marched to MARESQUEL where it entrained for BETHUNE. 4th (?) R.D.G. remounted to Hospital. The Coy. was joined at MARESQUEL by the Royals and N.S.Y. Coys. Battalion commenced entraining at 5.50 a.m. Train left station at 9.15 a.m. Battalion arrived FOUQUEREIL station at 12.15 p.m. then marched to billets in the Orphanage, BETHUNE, arriving about 1.30 p.m. 6th Battalion (3 D.G. Coy., I.R.D. Coy., N.S.Y. Coy.) in billets at BETHUNE	

Army Form C. 2118.

WAR DIARY
or
INTELLIGENCE SUMMARY

(Erase heading not required.)

3rd Dragoon Guards

Jan 1916

Instructions regarding War Diaries and Intelligence Summaries are contained in F. S. Regs., Part II. and the Staff Manual respectively. Title pages will be prepared in manuscript.

Hour, Date, Place	Summary of Events and Information	Remarks and references to Appendices
5.1.16 SAILLY-LA-BOURSE	The 1st Dismounted Batt in billets, late in the day orders were received that the Batt was to return to BETHUNE.	JHG
6.1.16 "	The Batt paraded at 10.30 AM and marched back to BETHUNE arriving about 11.30 AM. It went into billets in the Orphanage.	JHG
7.1.16 BETHUNE	Reserve billets	JHG
8.1.16 "	The Batt remains in Reserve billets. A reinforcement of 6 OR & 1 L.O. Horses joins the Regt at OFFIN. from ROUEN.	JHG
9.1.16 "	The Batt, less MG detachments, parades at 8.30 am The 3rd D.Gds Coy and that of the Royal Dragoons march to LA BOURSE where the Royals went into billets. The Batt HQ (3rd D.Gs), 3rd D.Gs. Coy and N.S.Y Coy proceeded to VERMELLES, and took over the reserve line of trenches (LANCASHIRE TRENCH)	JHG
10.1.16	Remains in LANCASHIRE TRENCH.	JHG

Army Form C. 2118.

WAR DIARY
or
INTELLIGENCE SUMMARY
(Erase heading not required.)

Instructions regarding War Diaries and Intelligence Summaries are contained in F. S. Regs., Part II. and the Staff Manual respectively. Title pages will be prepared in manuscript.

Hour, Date, Place	Summary of Events and Information	Remarks and references to Appendices
11.1.16. VERMELLES.	The Battn commenced to relieve the 8th Battn in the front line at 8.30 a.m., 7442 Pte VOLLER being killed, and 7015 PTE CORLETT wounded. 2/Lieut G.R.B. HARRIES discharge discharged to Hospital, 2/Lieut W. BLACK Capt HOLROYD-SMYTH & 2/Lt HARRIES left the Regt at OFFIN to join the Dismounted Battn	WAG WAG
12.1.16. D/ Section front line.	The Battn was in front line. Capt Holroyd-Smyth & 2/Lieut Harries joined Battn.	WAG
13.1.16.	Nothing of interest occurred.	WAG
14.1.16. (11.30 am)	Enemy fired an aerial Torpedo, greatly damaging KAISERIN TRENCH.	WAG
15.1.16.	At 10 am the Battn the Battn 2 Battn aus marren was relieved. To BETHUNE arriving there at 2 pm.	WAG
16.1.16	Battn was in Reserve billets in Bethune	WAG
17.1.16	Battn refitted.	WAG

Army Form C. 2118.

WAR DIARY
or
INTELLIGENCE SUMMARY

(Erase heading not required.)

Instructions regarding War Diaries and Intelligence Summaries are contained in F. S. Regs., Part II. and the Staff Manual respectively. Title pages will be prepared in manuscript.

Hour, Date, Place	Summary of Events and Information	Remarks and references to Appendices
18.1.16. BETHUNE.	HQ 1 Royal Dragoons arrived, and took over for duties of Batter HQ from 3DG'ds HQ at 12 A.M.	
19.1.16. "	HQ 3DG'ds entrained at BETHUNE at 2.30 pm for BEAURAINVILLE, arriving 8.2 pm. 1 star horses were waiting.	JWAG.
20.1.16 OFFIN	Daily Routine in billets.	JWAG
24.1.16 "	"	JWAG
22.1.16 "	A Reinforcement of 8 O.R. joined from Rouen.	JWAG
23.1.16 "	Routine in billets.	JWAG
24.1.16 "	"	JWAG
25.1.16 "	"	
26.1.16 "	"	
27.1.16 "	Composite Sqdn parades at OFFIN.	JWAG
28.1.16 "	Daily Routine.	JWAG
29.1.16 "	Staff Ride for all Officers ( ). Commander's Officer.	JWAG
30.1.16 "	Daily Routine in billets under Commander's Officer.	JWAG
31.1.16 "	Daily Routine.	JWAG

1247 W 3299 200,000 (E) 8/14 J.B.C. & A. Forms/C. 2118/11.

Army Form C. 2118.

WAR DIARY
or
INTELLIGENCE SUMMARY

(Erase heading not required.)

Instructions regarding War Diaries and Intelligence Summaries are contained in F. S. Regs., Part II. and the Staff Manual respectively. Title pages will be prepared in manuscript.

Hour, Date, Place	Summary of Events and Information	Remarks and references to Appendices
1 February. OFFIN.	Daily Routine in Billets. Dismounted Coy at BÉTHUNE	WAR
2nd " "	All remounts received during period 15-1-16 — 2-2-16 inspected by G.O.C. at HESMOND. Dismounted Coy went into trenches. Following Officers joined from Base at: F.B: KATINAKIS. 2/Lieuts G. & S. TENISON G. BRIGGS.	WAR
3rd " "	Composite Sqdn parades at OFFIN for training. Daily Routine	WAR.
4th " "	"	WAR.
5th " "	Dismounted Coy relieves in front line trenches. Daily Routine.	WAR.
6th " "	"	WAR.
8th " "	Composite Sqdn parades for training. Daily Routine.	WAR.
9th " "	Corps Commander inspects remounts that has joined per during period 15-1-16 — 2-2-16. Dismounted Coy relieved to permanent billets.	WAR.
10th " "		
11 " "		
12th " "	Reinforcements of 10. O.R. arrives from ROUEN.	WAR.
13th " "	Dismounted Coy refitted.	WAR.

WAR DIARY
or
INTELLIGENCE SUMMARY

(Erase heading not required.)

Army Form C. 2118.

Instructions regarding War Diaries and Intelligence Summaries are contained in F.S. Regs., Part II. and the Staff Manual respectively. Title pages will be prepared in manuscript.

Hour, Date, Place	Summary of Events and Information	Remarks and references to Appendices
14th February. OFFIN.	Daily Routine.	MAG.
15" "	" "	MAG.
16"	Inspection by Commanding Officer of "B" Sqn in marching order.	MAG.
17"	A Sqdn. inspected by Commanding Officer.	MAG.
18"	C Sqn in marching order inspected by Com'd Officer	MAG.
19"	MG Section inspected by Com'd Officer. 2/Lieut Sykes re joined from attachment to 1 Lieut Morton 1st Army.	MAG.
20"	Daily Routine.	MAG.
21"	Com'd Officer inspected "B" Sqdn in marching order.	
22"	" " "A" "	MAG
23"	" " "C" "	
24"	Training by Squadrons.	
25"	" " "	MAG
26"	" " "	
27"	Daily Routine and reinforcement 8.15 O.R. joined from ROUEN.	MAG
28"	Daily Routine.	
29"	B.M.G. Squadron formed. MG Section 309 transferred to GMG Sqdn. MAG "B" Sqn went of OFFIN. Vacated to make room for MG.Sqdn. moved to BEAURAINVILLE	MAG

Army Form C. 2118.

WAR DIARY
or
INTELLIGENCE SUMMARY
(Erase heading not required.)

Instructions regarding War Diaries and Intelligence Summaries are contained in F. S. Regs., Part II. and the Staff Manual respectively. Title pages will be prepared in manuscript.

Hour, Date, Place	Summary of Events and Information	Remarks and references to Appendices
1 March OFFIN	Daily Routine in Billets.	WAB
2" "	Training by Sqdns.	WAB
3" "	Squadron Training. In the evening, the Divisional Chaplain gave a Cinematograph entertainment in the Schoolroom at OFFIN.	WAB
4" "	Squadron Training. All whels transport inspected by Brigade Transport Officer at 2.15 pm at LOISON.	WAB
5" "	Sqdn Training.	WAB
6" "	Billets. 2/Lieuts Vincent & Savage promoted Lieuts.	WAB
7" "	Sqdn Training. Captain Carnegy re-joined Regt from HQ 3CavDiv.	WAB
8" "	The Regiment was inspected in marching order by the General Campbell Cmndg 6th Cav Bde. Sqdns and 'A' 2Echelon paraded at intervals of half an hour owing to limited space of drill ground. Routine in Billets.	WAB
9" "		
10" "	Regt carried out a Tactical Exercise at BOIS JEAN. 2/Lieut M.J.CLEARY & 23141 L/Cpl JACKSON proceeded to FRUGES to undergo a course of Signalling.	WAB
11" "	Daily Routine. 8 Seven O.R. joined from ROUEN	WAB
12" "	Daily Routine.	WAB

WAR DIARY or INTELLIGENCE SUMMARY

Army Form C. 2118.

Hour, Date, Place	Summary of Events and Information	Remarks and references to Appendices
13th March OFFIN	Lieut BOWLER proceeded to FIXECOURT, 3rd Army Sch. for a weeks instruction in trayner fighting.	WAG
14th March "	Sqdn Training. A & B Sqdn divided wagons paraded at Royon Sqdn Training. B & C HQ's backed in accordance with instructions issued.	WAG
15th "		WAG
16th "	Regt paraded for a Route March, left in marching order at 9.15 am. and marched to MONTREUIL via MARENLA, MARLES-Y-NEUVILLE, and returning by BEAUMAIRE, BRIMEUX & LESPINOY and BEAURAINVILLE arriving back in billets at 2 pm. Squadron Training. Divisional Sch of Scout opened at THRAMCOURT. Lts WOOLF, BENTON, VINCENT, & LONGBOTHAM and seven O.R. proceed to Div Sch of Scout.	WAG
17th "		WAG
18th "	Sqdn Training.	WAG
19th "	Routine in Billets. Divine Service at LOISON at 11 am.	WAG
20th "	Staff ride for Regimental Commanders and Sqdn Leaders to He Qr Car B.D. under General Campbell	WAG

Army Form C. 2118.

WAR DIARY
or
INTELLIGENCE SUMMARY

(Erase heading not required.)

Instructions regarding War Diaries and Intelligence Summaries are contained in F.S. Regs., Part II. and the Staff Manual respectively. Title pages will be prepared in manuscript.

Hour, Date, Place	Summary of Events and Information	Remarks and references to Appendices
21. March OFFIN	Tactical Exercise in marching order at SEMPY. ARMOURER-SERGEANT SUTTON proceeded to Machine Gun School at WISQUES to undergo instruction in Vickers Gun. Capt. T.G. Cliff appointed Temp. Major.	HQS.
22" " "	Routine in Billets.	HQS
23rd " "	Tactical Exercise carried out at SEMPY. General Vaughan, Comd 3 Cav. Div attended.	HQS.
24" " "	Sqn arrangements. Comd Officers gave a lecture to Officers & Sergeants on the previous day's scheme.	HQS
25" " "	Inspection of horses prepared for casting.	HQS
26" " "	Routine in Billets. Divine Service at LOISON at 10 A.M. 2/Lieut M.J. CLEARY & 4 men rejoined from Signalling Course.	HQS
27" " "	Regimental Tactical Exercise took Place at SEMPY. 3 officers and 7 OR. rejoined from Divisional School.	HQS

Army Form C. 2118.

WAR DIARY
or
INTELLIGENCE SUMMARY.
(Erase heading not required.)

Hour, Date, Place	Summary of Events and Information	Remarks and references to Appendices
March 28. OFFIN.	OC. A.S.C. 3rd Cav Div inspects the transport of the Regt in marching Order (A & B) Echelon.	NA9
29.	6th Cavalry Bde less 6 Cav Field Ambulance and B Echelon marching order parade. Rendez-vour at T Roads 500 yds N of the Q in OFFIN. (ARRAS 1/80000). The Bde moves along the following route. EMBRY – RIMBOVAL – MAISONCELLE–CRECY	NA8
30 – OFFIN.	Lieut. M.H. Dutson takes over duties of Sniping officer.	NA8 NA9
31 –	Billets. Capt. T.S. Kirigham admitted to Hospital.	NA9

3rd Dragoon Guards.

Appendices to War Diary.

Appendix I.   Pages. 1-2.
"   II.   "   3.
"   III.   "   4.
"   IV.   "   5-8.

APPENDIX I

Report on Operations
Nov. 5th & 6th.

At 5:30 p.m. the Regiment paraded at their bivouac near WITTEPORT and marched through ZOOGE and took over the trenches on the Eastern front of HERONTHAGE WOODS at 10 p.m.

B squadron on the right
A -   -   -   - Centre with maxim
C -   -   -   - Left with maxim

The Germans were in very close proximity and there was a good deal of rifle fire at different times during the night but no actual concerted attack was made.

At dawn on Nov. 6th an attack was repulsed Between 9 a.m. - 10 a.m. and 12 noon - 2 p.m. attacks were made and successfully repulsed, previous to these attacks the shelling was extremely heavy.

The right of the line was strengthened by 2 troops of the 1st Royal Dragoons and two maxims.

At 4 p.m. there was continuous very heavy shelling followed by an attack which was driven off.

There were further attacks as usual preceded by heavy shell fire at 7 p.m. & 12 m.n. which were also repulsed. The enemy must have suffered severely and our casualty list was

was also heavy.
Capt Kevill-Davies wounded
" Hodgkinson " — (since dead)
Lt Talbot " —
20 N.C.O.s & men killed
24 " " " wounded
                    Total 57.

We were relieved by the 5th Fusiliers at 2 a.m. 7th Nov. but they were unable to hold the enemy off.
The Regt reached bivouac at 6 a.m. on 7th.
The heavy casualties were due to some extent to the novelty of a Cavalry Regt being used in trenches and to the fact that they were taken somewhat unawares by the heavy shell fire.

O.B. Brigham
Lt. Colonel
Comg 3rd Dragoon Guards

Appendix II
Operations 8th 9th Nov.

At 5 p.m. 250 men of A, B & C Squadrons moved off from bivouac and took over support & reserve trenches situated about 1 mile S.E. of ZILLEBEKE.

Though there was a considerable amount of activity in the fire & forward trenches, the 3rd Dragoon Guards were not called upon for action.

O.B. Bingham
Lt. Col
Cmdg 3rd Dragoon Guards

Appendix III
Report on operations Nov. 12th 13th

At 3 pm the Regiment moved off dismounted from Bivouac near HALTE and took up a position about 1 mile due East of ZILLEBEKE in support of Lord Cavans trenches. We were not then called upon for action.

At 5 pm the Regt moved up to the trenches about 1 mile S.E of ZILLEBEKE. With the exception of a little shelling and sniping the night passed quietly. There was every indication that a heavy attack would be made at dawn on the 13th Nov. but all was quiet until 8.30 am when there was some very heavy shelling & Lieut Talbot was reported killed about 9.30 am, the trenches having been attacked in some force but successfully repulsed. The maxim guns were put out of action by the heavy fire of the enemy.

The Regt was relieved by the Royal Horse Guards about 6.30 pm & returned to Bivouac.

Casualties — Lieut Talbot killed
5 N.C.O's & men —
15 " " — Wounded
Total 26.

O.B. Bingham
Lt Colonel
Cmg 3rd Dragoon Guards

Appendix IV.

REPORT ON OPERATIONS.   15. 16. 17. Nov.

On Sunday Nov. 15th the 3rd Dragoon Guards and two Squadrons of the North Somerset Yeomanry were ordered to take over the trenches situated directly on the Eastern side of the ZILLEBEKE - KLEINZILLEBEKE ROAD. The trenches were taken over from the 1st Life Guards 7.30 p.m.

   B Squadron 3rd Dragoon Guards on the right.
   A   "   North Somerset Yeo. centre.
   C   "   3rd Dragoon Guards on the left.
   A   "   3rd Dragoon Guards were in support.
   B   "   North Somerset Yeo. in reserve.

The night of the 15th - 16th Nov. passed quietly only a certain amount of sniping being noticeable.

On the morning of the 16th shortly after daybreak the trenches were heavily shelled - shelling continued more or less severely practically the whole day, but there was very little rifle fire during the day.

At 8 p.m. having previously received instructions that we were to remain on duty in the same trenches for another 24 hours I effected the following reliefs

A Squadron 3.D.G. moved up into the fire trenches on the right of my line in relief of B Squad'n 3 D.G. who fell back to the support trenches.

B. Squadron North Somerset Yeomanry took over the fire trenches of their A Squadron who retired to the reserve trenchs.

C Squadron 3. D.G. remaining in their fire trenches on the left of the line.

At 8.30 p.m. and 11.45 p.m. there was some heavy rifle fire chiefly on the left of the line. The remainder of the night passed quietly except for a considerable amount of sniping.

At 9 a.m. on the 17th very heavy - continuous gun fire was brought to bear on all the trenches and the whole area was subject to a terrific shelling. Shortly after the commencement of this heavy fire my Regt. Serjeant Major (Mr Stewart) was killed by a shell.

At 1 p.m. the Germans attacked my line on the right & centre (A Squdn 3.D.G - B Squdn. N. Somerset Yeo.) coming on to within 20 yds. or so of the trenches. This attack was repulsed with heavy loss to the enemy, our shrapnel being very effective when the enemy retired. Shelling from the enemy's guns naturally slackening for the time being. After the repulse of this attack gun fire again broke out in great intensity and about 3·45 p.m. another attack developed this chiefly against the left of my line defended by C Squadron 3.D.G who suffered heavily in the loss of officers & men. I was able to move up 2 troops of B Squadⁿ 3.D.G. to reinforce C. Squadⁿ 3.D.G. and I also moved up 2 troops of A Squadⁿ N. Somerset Yeo. into the support trenches and shortly afterwards moved the remaining two troops of B Squadⁿ. 3.D.G. into the fire trenches & brought the other two troops of A Sqdⁿ. N. Somerset Yeo. up to the support trenches, having under Lord Cavan's orders sent for the Coldstream Guards to come up to form the reserve. On arrival of the Coldstreams I reinforced the firing line with 30 men of A Squadⁿ N. Somerset Yeo. The attack which was very determined was repulsed. The loss to the enemy cannot be estimated as dusk was coming on but it must have been heavy.

Situated in the vicinity of Captain Wright's trenches (C Squadⁿ. 3. D.G. left of line) was a farm building. Some Germans got possession of it. Three times it was attacked by C Sqdn. at the third attempt which was led by Capt. Wright possession of it was gained Captain Wright himself shooting 4 Germans with his revolver.

The trenches were taken over about 7.30 p.m by the 7th Cavalry Brigade.

The casualties of the force under my command for the 48 hours consisted of

Capt. Wright 3.D.G killed
" Stewart " wounded } C Sqdn.
Lt. Chapman " wounded (since dead) } 3.D.G.
Capt. F. Liebert B Squadn N. Som. Yeo. killed
Lt. J. Davey " "
Lt. J. Bailward A " " wounded
Capt.-Adjt. S.G. Bates (7th Hussars)
N.C.Os - Men 3.D.G. 11 killed 41 wounded
"   N.Som.Y 21 "   27
        Total   32 killed   68 wounded.

Where all did so well it is hard to particularise and the N. Somerset Yeo. were very steady under fire - behaved gallantly.

    B. Bingham
    Lt. Colonel
    Cmg. 3rd Dragoon Guards

3 Cd
6 CB

War Diary
3rd Dragoon Guards

12.13.4.4
15.9.84

April 1916.

Confidential

WAR DIARY
or
INTELLIGENCE SUMMARY.

Army Form C. 2118.

3rd Dragoon Guards

April 1916.

Place	Date	Hour	Summary of Events and Information	Remarks and references to Appendices
April	1		Horse inspection by G.O.C at LOISON.	
	2	OFFIN.	Billets. G. OR joined from ROUEN.	
	3		Billets.	WA9
	4		Billets.	WA9
	5		Billets.	
	6		The Regiment carried out a wood-scheme in Bois d'HESDIN. All transport driven were lectured to by Bde Transport Officer.	
	7		The DADR inspected all Covers of RAYON.	

Army Form C. 2118.

WAR DIARY
or
INTELLIGENCE SUMMARY

(Erase heading not required.)

Instructions regarding War Diaries and Intelligence Summaries are contained in F. S. Regs., Part II. and the Staff Manual respectively. Title pages will be prepared in manuscript.

Hour, Date, Place	Summary of Events and Information	Remarks and references to Appendices
April 8-4-16 OFFN.	LIEUT. C. H. NEWTON-DEAKIN admitted to Hospital/	/AG
9-4-16.	Work in billets.	
10-4-16.	" " "	/AG
11-4-16.	" " "	/AG
12-4-16.	Regt Staff Ride for Officers.	/AG
13-4-16	Routine in Billets.	/AG
14-4-16	" "	
15-4-16.	G.O.C. Bde inspects horses of B'tt Salns & Platoon & No. 4 Coy 'A' at LOISON.	/AG
16-4-16.	LIEUT BAGNELL and sixteen other ranks joined from ROUEN.	/AG
17-4-16.	Routine in Billets.	/AG
18-4-16	Regt Route march to ESTREE. Advance Party proceeds to ETAPLES to over camp.	/AG
19-4-16	Routine in Billets. Regt Staff ride	/AG
20-4-16	" "	/AG
21-4-16	" "	/AG

1247 W 3299 200,000 (E) 8/14 J.B.&C. & A. Forms/C. 2118/11.

Army Form C. 2118.

WAR DIARY
or
INTELLIGENCE SUMMARY.
(Erase heading not required.)

Hour, Date, Place			Summary of Events and Information	Remarks and references to Appendices
April.	22.	OFFIN.	Routine in Billets	WAR
	23"	"	Routine in Billets.	WAR
	24"	"	Training Camp Postpned owing to Outbreak of Mumps	WAR
	25"	"	Routine in Billets	WAR
	26"	"	Boxing Tournament held by Division at Fauges.	WAR
	27"	"	Pyrwood - selem in FORET D'HESDIN.	WAR
	28.	"	Routine in Billets.	WAR
	29.		LIEUT. G.R. ALSOP joined from Base.	WAR
	30		Routine in Billets	WAR

WAR DIARY or INTELLIGENCE SUMMARY

Army Form C. 2118.

3rd Dragoon Guards

May 1916

Place	Date	Hour	Summary of Events and Information	Remarks and references to Appendices
May.	2		[Routine with Units]	
	3		" " "	
	4		" " "	
			Routine in billets	
			Gallant conduct of Pte THEWLIS. C Sqdn recommended diving fully clothed into the River GANCHE by reserving the child from drowning. Supposed his to hospital suffering from exhaustion. He was admitted	
	5		Routine in billets	
	6		Routine in billets	

WAR DIARY
or
INTELLIGENCE SUMMARY

(Erase heading not required.)

Army Form C. 2118

Place	Date	Hour	Summary of Events and Information	Remarks and references to Appendices
OFFIN	10-5-16	—	Routine in Billets	WAR
"	11-5-16	—	Routine in Billets	WAR
"	12-5-16	—	Routine in Billets	WAR
"	13-5-16	—	Routine in Billets. Regimental Dinner.	WAR
"	14-5-16	—	Lieut-Col Nellis, Major Bower, Major Cardwell, Royal Canadian Dragoons joins Regt for Div Manoeuvres at Abbeville.	WAR
"	15-5-16	—	Fighting Troops and Establ'mt of the Regt joins Bde at BEAURAINVILLE and marches to ST RIQUIER for Divisional Training, Regiment was billeted in ONEUX	WAR
ST RIQUIER	16-5-16	—	Bde Training 6 am – 10 am	WAR
"	17-5-16	—	Bde Training 2 pm – 6 pm	WAR
"	18-5-16	—	Tactical Exercise under G.O.C Reserve Corps.	WAR
"	19-5-16	—	Bde Training 7 am – 11 am	WAR
"	20-5-16	—	10 BR and 1 Cav Bde joined from ROUEN. Tactical Exercise under G.O.C Division. 6th Cav Bde under Lieut-Col Q Bert	WAR
"	21-5-16	—	Capt. Nicholson R.V.C. joined. Regiment paraded at 6-30 am and marched back to OFFIN arriving about 8-30 pm.	WAR
OFFIN	22-5-16	—	Routine in Billets	WAR
"	23-5-16	—	Routine in Billets. Lieut-Col AEW HARMAN 2nd Drgs assumes command 6th Cav Bde	WAR
PARIS PLAGE	24-5-16	—	The Regt moves to PARIS PLAGE via MARENLA & NEUVILLE.	WAR
PARIS PLAGE	25-5-16	—	Regimental Drill on the shore	WAR
"	26-5-16	—	General Vaughan inspects the Camp and the billets en route to Rmy Hd Qrs the Colonel has expressed pleased with the Regt.	WAR

Army Form C. 2118

WAR DIARY
or
INTELLIGENCE SUMMARY
(Erase heading not required.)

Instructions regarding War Diaries and Intelligence Summaries are contained in F. S. Regs, Part II. and the Staff Manual respectively. Title Pages will be prepared in manuscript.

Place	Date	Hour	Summary of Events and Information	Remarks and references to Appendices
PARIS PLAGE	27-5-16		Bath and Regimental Training.	N/AS
	28-5-16		Commanding Officer inspects the Camp.	N/AS
	29-5-16		Tactical Exercise.	N/AS
	30-5-16		Dismounted Work, musketry & Drill.	
	31-5-16		Routine in Camp.	N/AS
	1-6-16		Regt Scheme. Lieut E.A. Newton-Deakin joined from Hospital.	
	2-6-16		Field Firing Scheme.	N/AS
	3-6-16		Routine in Camp. General Vaughan present.	N/AS
			Jumping Competition for Officers was won by Lieut Harris 3" D. Gds. Open Jumping Competition for NCO's was won by the N.C.O's jumping.	
	4-6-16		Camp inspected by Commanding Officer.	N/AS
	5-6-16		Routine in Camp.	N/AS
	6-6-16		2/Lieuts R.D. Younger & Cleaver and R. Noman joined from Base.	N/AS
OFF'N	7-6-16		Regiment marched from Camp to permanent billets via NEUVILLE.	N/AS
	8 "		Routine in billets.	
	9 "			
	11 "		11 Other Ranks Joined from Rouen.	
	12 "		In Preparation for Div Training.	
	13.		Divisional Training Camsells	

1875 Wt. W593/826 1,000,000 4/15 J.B.C. & A. A.D.S.S./Forms/C. 2118.

WAR DIARY
or
INTELLIGENCE SUMMARY
(Erase heading not required.)

Army Form C. 2118

Instructions regarding War Diaries and Intelligence Summaries are contained in F.S. Regs., Part II. and the Staff Manual respectively. Title Pages will be prepared in manuscript.

Place	Date	Hour	Summary of Events and Information	Remarks and references to Appendices
OFFIN.	14-6-16		2/Lieut M.J. Clery assumes duties of Signalling Officer. Routine in billets.	WA3
	15.		Line advances on hour. Routine in Billets	WA3
	16		R.S.M. Cordwell promoted 2/Lieut and posted to Regt.	WA3
	17.		Aeroplane rope par[ty] in Div Reserve.	WA3
	18.		Lieut A.B.P.L. Vincent awarded the Military Cross. 1085 Sgt Twist — — Military medal. Lt-Col. A. Burt mentioned in despatches & given a lever Lt-Colonelcy. 3777 S.S.M. Buxton mentioned in despatches.	WA3
	19.		Inspection of troops horses by G.O.C. 6th Cav Bde. 2/Lt Clay's troop selected as best troop.	WA3
	20. 21. 22. 23.		Routine in Billets — · —	WA3

Army Form C. 2118

WAR DIARY
or
INTELLIGENCE SUMMARY
(Erase heading not required.)

Place	Date	Hour	Summary of Events and Information	Remarks and references to Appendices
OFFIN	24-6-16		The Regt complete with transport proceeded to the Bde Rendez vous Tracks 220 405 B P in Pt ST VAAST (1/100,000 ABEVILLE) at 8-15 pm the 6th Cav Bde then marched to MARCHEVILLE, via HESDIN - REGNAUVILLE - LABROYE. The Regiment went into bivouac. Strength: |	Officers	OR	Horses	Wagons | |---|---|---|---|---| | Fighting troops | 23 | 380 | 433 | | | A Echelon | 01 | 71 | 109 | 10 | | B " | 01 | 25 | 24 | 5 | | Total | 24 | 476 | 566 | 15 |	
MARCHEVILLE	2-5-16		The Regiment remains in bivouac until 7pm when it moves to the Bde rendez vous at the X roads 700 yds N of the X in YVRENCHEUX joining the 6th Cav Bde at 9pm. The dismounted Coy, strength 2 officers 99 men, which has remained behind in WILLE entrains at BEAUVOIRVILLE at 2-30 pm & proceeds to ST. LEGER-LES-DOMART arriving at 9pm. The Regiment marches into the same place about 12 midnight.	

WAR DIARY or INTELLIGENCE SUMMARY

Army Form C. 2118

Place	Date	Hour	Summary of Events and Information	Remarks and references to Appendices
R.DOMART.	26		The dismounted Sqdn entrained at 4pm & BONNAY arriving about 10pm. The Regiment joins 6th Cav Bde at the NW entrance to VIGNACOURT at 9.30pm.	
	27		Marched to BONNAY via FLESSELLES — ALLONVILLE — QUERRIEU — BONNAY — BERTANGLES. The Bde then went into bivouac in the Bois ESCARD about 5am. The weather was very bad, raining continuing throughout the night.	WAR
BONNAY.	28		In bivouac at BONNAY Sqdn.	
	29		ALBERT to see country and being carried on against enemy front line trenches.	WAR
	30		Sqdn leaves & N.C.O's used to ride to bombardment that was, at the	WAR
	1-7-16			WAR
F-16.	2nd		The Regiment was turned out ready to move at 7-15am in the meanwhile reports Bois ESCARDONNEUSE with Echelon "A". At 10 am the Regt Off/Saddles became in & the ⊗ Infantry's progress. At 6pm the Regiment was ordered back to bivouac 1 Officer, 1 5 O.R. arrives from Base. Divine Service for R.C.'s held at BONNAY Church at 8am, 1 pm C of E afterwards.	WAR WAR

WAR DIARY
INTELLIGENCE SUMMARY

3rd D. Gds Army Form C. 2118

Vol 18

Place	Date	Hour	Summary of Events and Information	Remarks and references to Appendices
BONNAY.	3-7-16		Reinforcements of 14 O.R. was joined from Base. The Regt Orders to stand to at 4 hours from 9 am. As afton orders were received that the Regt was probably move back towards Allonville.	WAG
	4-7-16		The Regt paraded at 5-15 am and marched off with the Bde to MEERLESART VIA OLUIEU & PICQUIGNY.	
MEERLESART	5-7-16		2/Lieut G Briggs and SQMS Young and 50 OR proceeded to LONDPRE when the entraining party was executing was to MERICOURT to work under the XV Corps. This Capt C W Brunner was to the XV corps to clear the battle field. The Regiment rejoined the Regiment from Canterbury.	WAG
	6-7-16		Capt Holroyd-Smyth rejoined the Regiment from Bonne Bay. The Commanding Officer, Brig-General Q.E.W. Harman who was present had a staff ride for officers in the afternoon.	WAG
	7-7-16		Orders were received to the effect that the Regiment was to be prepared to move at 1 1/2 hrs notice from 6 am the next day. This order was cancelled during the day	WAG 11A Gunshee her i/s3/3 3a D.Gds.
	8-7-16		The Regiment was warned that it would probably move back to the neighbourhood of QUERRIEU after 1pm. The dismounted party then received orders to pause of men and march to hourpre, the Regt to rendez-vous on the eastern outskirts b Ciraures.	WAG

WAR DIARY
INTELLIGENCE SUMMARY
(Erase heading not required.)

Army Form C. 2118

Place	Date	Hour	Summary of Events and Information	Remarks and references to Appendices
MEERLES ART	8-7-16		The Regt marched with Bde to CORBIE, arrived about 5-30pm on the 9th. Horse lines were in lowlying ground by the River Somme.	WAR
	9-7-16		The Dismounted Party arrives about 1pm, also GOR who joined from Rouen. During the afternoon Orders were received saying that the Bde was now to march to another area. The Regiment marches independently to VAUX-SUR-SOMME and arrived about 6 P.M. and went into bivouac on the banks of the canal de la SOMME. The Dismounted Party remained at CORBIE and was attached to 2nd L.Gds.	WAR
	10-7-16		The Regiment remained in bivouac at Vaux. The Regt was placed under 2hrs notice.	WAR
	11-7-16		In Bivouac	WAR
	12-7-16		In Bivouac at Vaux, Regt under 4 hrs notice	WAR
	13-7-16		In Bivouac	WAR
	13-7-16		Orders were received to the effect that the Regiment was to be ready to move off within ½ hr. The next day orders were saddle up 4 a.m.	WAR
	14-7-16		The Regiment was Saddled up at 4 a.m. but off saddled at 7 a.m. and stood to at 8pm the stag to remain was cancelled for the night. Q Park Horses from Base to complete Hotchkiss Detachment. 3 O.R. + 12 Riding horses also taken on the strength.	WAR
	15-7-16		The Regt stood to from 5am at ½ hr notice. This was eventually cancelled at 10-15pm from 6am 1½ hr from 6am. The Regt carried out a marching order	WAR
	16-7-16			WAR

WAR DIARY
INTELLIGENCE SUMMARY
(Erase heading not required.)

Army Form C. 2118

Place	Date	Hour	Summary of Events and Information	Remarks and references to Appendices
VAUX - SUR - SOMME	16.7.16		parade. O.C.n.g.S. Service was held in camp. No 577) S.S.M Buxton awarded the military Cross. The Regt was placed on 4 hrs notice later in the day. Lieut. M.P. Noel returned to Regt duty from employment with C.M.G. Sqdn and was posted to A Sqdn.	WAE
	17.7.16		The Regiment remained in Bivouac at VAUX.	WAE
	18.7.16		The Regiment was ordered to be ready to move into a new billeting area.	WAE
	19.7.16		The nucleus of the dismounted party was carried out. 2/Lieut M.V.T. Mott replacing 2/Lieut G. Briggs in charge of the party. During the afternoon the Regt marched independently to LA NEUVILLE and went into bivouac about 6 P.M. During this period the Regt was at 4 hrs notice.	WAE
LA NEUVILLE.	20.7.16		O.C. 6 Cav. Field Ambulance carried out a medical inspection of the men in the Regt.	WAE
	21.7.16		Brig-General Norman Com'd'g Cav. Bde carried out a Staff Ride for Comm'd Officers & in Command's, Adjutants, in the morning. during the afternoon the Comm'd Officer held the same Ride for Sqdn leaders. Major G.T. ceyl Pries to Staff ride for Hotchkiss and Scout Officers. Divine Service for C.n.g & I.R.C. at 11 a.m.	WAE
	22.7.16.		Routine in bivouac.	WAE
	23.7.16 24.7.16		The Regt carried out an outpost scheme in marching order. The Regt was ordered to find a working party in the 4th C.A. Tench 2nd 1.95 O.R. During the evening the Regt gave a coker in the working party details an orders joined the Regt in Corps for salvage work, and for the defence of CONTALMAISON.	WAE

Lt. Langlotan
G.Cockwell

J.R.Quiclot 2/3/21
7 oyl ot O.C.
Dago 10
1 GSL
2 GS
12
96

WAR DIARY or INTELLIGENCE SUMMARY

Army Form C. 2118

Place	Date	Hour	Summary of Events and Information	Remarks and references to Appendices
LA NEUVILLE.	26.7.		Regt Working Party of 1 Officer & 16 O.R. joining Regt Raving Works under 3rd Div. 1 Officer & 3 O.R. rejoining from digging at Bécourt. Quarter Park, 2 Off & 880 R. proceed to Bécourt to work under III Corps.	WAR
	27.7.		8 Rgg D1 light Draught Horse joining from Base.	WAR.
	28.7.		R.S.O.C. has a tactical tour. The following Officers attend: — Lieut-Col. A. Bew. Major G.T. Cayley. Lieut. W.A. Quinlan, Capt Conway. Capt. Worthington, Capt Rotary Smyth.	WAR.
	29.7.			WAR.
	30.7.		A relief of Part of the Working Party was carried out 2nd Lieut R.D. Younger relieved 2nd Lieut Q.R.P. Alsop off OR Senensé. Horses 82. Wagon 1. This party paraded at La Neuville at 11.45 am 42 O.R. 4 cycles - moved, mounted to Bécourt. During the evening orders were received that the Division would move in a westerly direction, later all orders were cancelled and digging party received.	
	31.7.		All digging parties returned. The Regiment was turned up ready to move at 6 am and moved to LA MESGE. VIA VECQUEMONT. — AMIENS. — LA CHAUSSÉE - PICQUIGNY. — SOUES. Dismounted men moving at LA NEUVILLE incumbium to foresoring van to CAOURS at which place they arrived at 3.30 pm.	WAR
LA MESGE	1-8-16			WAR
	2-8-16		The Commanding Officer S Sgt. the Regiment left LA MESGE at 4-30 pm. Marks via SOUES. — PONT REMY to CAOURS arriving at 11-30 am.	WAR
CAOURS.	3-8-16		The G.O.C. saw all Commanding Officers and Squadron Leaders at 3.30 pm at MILLENCOURT.	WAR

Vague note 2/2/3 D.S.

Army Form C. 2118.

WAR DIARY
or
INTELLIGENCE SUMMARY.

(Erase heading not required.)

3rd Dragoon Guards

Title pages August 1916.

Place	Date	Hour	Summary of Events and Information	Remarks and references to Appendices
			Copied from preceding diary	
LA MESGE	1.8.16		The Regiment was formed up ready to move at 6 a.m., and moved to LA MESGE VIA VECQUEMONT — AMIENS — LA CHAUSSÉE — PICQUIGNY — SOUES. Dismounted then remained at LA NEUVILLE but entrained the following day for CAOURS at which place they arrived at 3.30 p.m.	
	2.8.16		The Regiment left LA MESGE at 4.30 a.m. & marched via SOUES — PONT REMY to CAOURS arriving at 11.30 a.m.	
CAOURS	3.8.16		The G.O.C. saw all Commanding Officers and S/Ldr leaders at 3.30 p.m. at MILLENCOURT.	

Army Form C. 2118

3rd S.G.

Vol 19

WAR DIARY
or
INTELLIGENCE SUMMARY
(Erase heading not required.)

Place	Date	Hour	Summary of Events and Information	Remarks and references to Appendices
CAOURS.	4-8-16		The Regiment was formed up ready to move off at 4-15 a.m. and joined the 6th Cav. Bde. at MILLENCOURT, and proceeded to ROUSSENT. VIA, CRECY, MARCHEVILLE - AGECOURT. The dismounted party, under 1st Leninron entrained for BEAURAINVILLE at 1-30 p.m. and arrived about 8 P.M.	WAS
ROUSSENT.	5-8-16.		The Regt and 2nd Ldn. G.S. were formed up ready 10 men per the other at ROUSSENTAL, and marched independently to OFFIN.	WAS
OFFIN.	6-8-16		Church Service at 11 a.m. by C.of.E.	WAS
	7-8-16.		Routine in billets. 2.O.R. joined from base, ROUEN.	WAS H.Q Quartee de G.
	8-8-16.		Sgt Hicks and 2.O.R. attached 21st Div for sniping in front line with 64 Infantry Bde.	WAS
	9-8-16		4.O.O.R. proceeded to TORCY to keep field Sqdn 10 groom horses as latter has to send 40 men to work under Reserve Army.	JWK JWS
	10-8-16		Routine in billets	JWK JWS
	11-8-16 12-8-16 13-8-16		Routine in billets 21 riding horses joined from Base Rouen. 8.O.R. joined from Rouen. 2 Officers and 60 O.R. proceed for work under II Corps	WAS JWS WAS

WAR DIARY
INTELLIGENCE SUMMARY
(Erase heading not required.)

Army Form C. 2118

Instructions regarding War Diaries and Intelligence Summaries are contained in F.S. Regs., Part II. and the Staff Manual respectively. Title Pages will be prepared in manuscript.

Place	Date	Hour	Summary of Events and Information	Remarks and references to Appendices
OFFIN.	14-8-16		Routine in billets.	
	15-8-16		Major and Temp Lieut-Col (Brevet Lieut-Col) A. Kent promotes Lieut-Col and to command 1st 3rd Dragoon Guards dates 2nd July 1916.	WAR
	16-8-16		G.O.C 6th Cavalry Bde inspects horses	WAR
			HESMOND. Tactical tour by Commanding Officer & Squn leaders	WAR
	17-8-16		Routine in billets.	WAR
	18-8-16		" " "	WAR
	19-8-16		Sniping Party attacks 21st Div. relieves by 3.O.R.	WAR
	20-8-16		Routine in billets	WAR
	21-8-16		The A.D.M.S. 3rd Cav. Div inspects the Medical and Sanitary arrangements	WAR
	22-8-16		of the Regt. 5.O.R joins from Rouen. Capt C.W. Brennand admitted to Hospital.	WAR
	23-8-16		Routine in billets	WAR
	24-8-16		" — —	WAR
	25-8-16		" — —	WAR
	26-8-16		G.O.C. inspects all Steel Knapsack of the Regt. Lieut. R.B. Allen rejoins from Sick leave in England.	WAR

H.Q. Quarter Master 3rd D.G

WAR DIARY
INTELLIGENCE SUMMARY
(Erase heading not required.)

Army Form C. 2118

Instructions regarding War Diaries and Intelligence Summaries are contained in F.S. Regs., Part II. and the Staff Manual respectively. Title Pages will be prepared in manuscript.

Place	Date	Hour	Summary of Events and Information	Remarks and references to Appendices
OFFIN-	27.8.16		8.O.R. joined from Rouen.	WD
	28.		Routine in billets.	WD
	29.		Tactical Exercise in conjunction with N.S.Y and "C" Battery, R.H.A. Major L. Ingham. Lieut E.A. Green, and Lieut G.L. Clarke, Yorkshire Dragoons attached for training.	WD
	30.		Routine in billets.	WD
	31.		Routine in billets. 1st Relief of Dismounted party was marching under Major O.T. Celf went up to take charge of II Corps carries out Divisional party.	WD

H.A Quintas Lieut.
3rd D.G's.

WAR DIARY or INTELLIGENCE SUMMARY

Army Form C. 2118

3rd Dragoon Guards

September 1916.

Place	Date	Hour	Summary of Events and Information	Remarks and references to Appendices
OFFIN.	1-9-16		Routine in billets. 2nd relief of dismounted party working under II Corps.	WPG
	2-9-16		Routine in billets.	WPG
	3-9-16		" "	WPG
	4-9-16		" "	WPG
	5-9-16		1 Cpl and 2 O.R. joined 21st Div. G.S. Sniping duties. Tactical Exercise between N.S. & D. Regt.	WPG
	6-9-16		Orders received for the Bde to be ready to move at about the 10th inst.	WPG
	7-9-16		All details attached to II Corps rejoined.	WPG
	8-9-16		Lieut. R.B. ALLEN proceeded to CAMIERS for a machine gun course.	WPG
	9.		Orders received to the effect that the Regt was to be ready to move on the 10th inst.	WPG
	10.		The Regiment with A & B Echelons paraded at BEAURAINVILLE at 10AM and marched to ARGOULES, via GOUY, ST. ANDRE and SAULCHOY arriving about 12 noon. The Regiment went into bivouac on the banks of the river L'AUTHIE.	WPG
	11.		Lieut. J. H. Sykes and 2/Lieut. G. BRIGGS and 71 O.R. forming the dismounted party remaining in bivouac at BEAURAINVILLE.	WPG
ARGOULES.			Lieut. D. H. OSMASTON admitted to Hospital.	WPG
			The Regiment with their Echelon assembled at the G.t roads S of LE PETIT CHEMIN at 2.5 pm and marched to LE PLESSEIL, via VIRONCHAUX – CRECY – FORET L'ABBAYE and arrived about 5.30pm and went into Bivouac in the higher	WPG
LE PLESSEIL	12		The Regiment assembled at the X roads 650 yds WNB Bois de L'ABBAYE. at 11.25 AM and marched to LA CHAUSSÉE via VAUCHELLES – FLIXECOURT arrived about 7pm.	WPG

WAR DIARY
or
INTELLIGENCE SUMMARY
(Erase heading not required.)

Army Form C. 2118

Instructions regarding War Diaries and Intelligence Summaries are contained in F. S. Regs., Part II. and the Staff Manual respectively. Title Pages will be prepared in manuscript.

Place	Date	Hour	Summary of Events and Information	Remarks and references to Appendices
LA CHAUSEE	13.9.16		The Bde remained in bivouac and was ordered to be ready to move again on the 14th inst	WAS.
N. of BUSSY	14.9.16		The Regiment arrived at the N end of ST.SAUVEUR at 8.15pm and marched to XAREA via CITADEL of AMIENS - RIVERY - CAMON. The Bde detrained at mid-day and then marched to a bivouac N of BUSSY. B.O.R. and 1 Charger joined from ROUEN.	WAS.
N of BONNAY	15.9.16		Orders were received that by 11 am the Division would be concentrated N of BONNAY, and was ready to move at 1/2 hrs notice after 11AM. At 8PM. Orders were received that the Regiment would move into bivouac for the night. 1 Sect. M.G. attached to Regt. MAJOR. G.T. CLIFF admitted to Hospital.	WAS.
	16.9.16		The Bde was under 2hrs notice to move from 9am. At 7-30 pm orders were received that the Bde was to move at 7.30 am the next day.	WAS.
	17.9.16		The Regiment was found up in bivouac or 7.15 am and marched to PONT. NOYELLES. Then went into bivouac. The weather was particularly bad night. 4 Sgts and 4 Cpls joined from ROUEN.	WAS.
PONT. NOYELLES	18.9.16		Remained in bivouac. Heavy rain.	WAS.
	19.		— ; — ; — ; — ; — ; — ; — ;	WAS.
	20.		Remained in bivouac. Heavy rain continued.	WAS.
	21.		— ; — ; — ; — ; Hostile aeroplanes dropped a few bombs on a neighbouring village during the night.	WAS.
	22		The Regiment fumed up to the Base line via AMIENS - PIC QUIGNY, and at 12-30pm and marched to LA NIESGE, via AMIENS - PIC QUIGNY, arrived about 5PM.	WAS. WAS. WAS.

1875 Wt. W593/826 1,000,000 4/15 J.B.C. & A. A.D.S.S./Forms/C. 2118.

WAR DIARY or **INTELLIGENCE SUMMARY**

3rd D.G'ds Vol 20

Army Form C. 2118

Place	Date	Hour	Summary of Events and Information	Remarks and references to Appendices
1.B.Mesge.	Sept. 23.		The Regiment paraded at 9 am and marched to WAVINS via FLIXECOURT, DOMART.	WAR
WAVINS.	24.		The Bde moved at 6.10 am to a new billeting area in the L'AUTHIE VALLEY. Bde H.Q being at DOURIEZ and Regt H.Q at MAINTENAY.	WAR
MAINTENAY.	25.		Remained in billets. Lieut. J.H. Sykes proceeded to Indian Army for attachment.	WAR
	26.		Routine in billets. Reinforcements of 5 O.R. and 11 Bdg horses joining from Rouen.	WAR / WAR
	27.		Routine in billets.	WAR
	28.		— ; — ; Lieut. J.H. Sykes struck off the strength.	WAR
	29.		— ; — ;	WAR
	30.		Routine in billets.	WAR

H.A. Quinton
Lieut. & 9/ass
3rd Dragoon Gds.

WAR DIARY or INTELLIGENCE SUMMARY

Army Form C. 2118

Place	Date	Hour	Summary of Events and Information	Remarks and references to Appendices
MAINTENAY	1-10-16		A Working Party of 2 two Officers and 46 O.R. was detailed for work under II Corps.	WAQ
" "	2-10-16		Capt. H.P. Noer and twent Q.R. Allen and 46 O.R. entrained at MAINTENAY and proceeded to BOUZINCOURT. 11 O.R. joined from ROUEN.	WAQ
" "	3-10-16		A Regimental Tactical Exercise in vicinity of billets.	WAQ
" "	4-10-16		Routine in billets.	WAQ
" "	5-10-16		" " "	WAQ
" "	6-10-16		Tactical Exercise against 1st Cav. Div. cancelled owing to bad weather.	WAQ
" "	7-10-16		The Regiment carried out another Scheme at MAINTENAY.	WAQ
" "	8-10-16		Routine in billets.	WAQ
" "	9-10-16		" " "	WAQ
" "	10-10-16		" " "	WAQ
" "	11-10-16		The Regiment took part in a Tactical Exercise with 2 Regts 107th Bn.	WAQ
" "	12-10-16		Scheme with M.G. Sqdn in vicinity of billets.	WAQ
" "	13-10-16		Routine in billets.	WAQ
" "	14-10-16		The Regiment and M.G. Sqdn carried out a Tactical Exercise in vicinity of billets.	WAQ
" "	15-10-16		Lieut Q.R.B. Monnie admitted to Hospital having been thrown from his horse.	WAQ
" "	16-10-16		Reinforcement of 8 O.R. joined from France.	WAQ
" "	17-10-16		Routine in billets.	WAQ
" "	18-10-16		Capt. N. M. Ferd Stone joined from England.	WAQ
" "	19-10-16		Routine in billets. Billeting Parties sent on to mobilizing area. CAMPNEUVILLES-LES-BRANDES.	WAQ
RANG DU FLIERS			AIRON-ST-VAAST-AIRON-NOTRE-DAME.	WAQ
" "	20-11-16		Lieut. Hellyer & 65 O.R. proceeded to BOUZINCOURT.	WAQ
			Capt. H.P. Noer and party returns from BOUZINCOURT.	WAQ

Army Form C. 2118

WAR DIARY
or
INTELLIGENCE SUMMARY
(Erase heading not required.)

Instructions regarding War Diaries and Intelligence Summaries are contained in F.S. Regs., Part II. and the Staff Manual respectively. Title Pages will be prepared in manuscript.

Place	Date	Hour	Summary of Events and Information	Remarks and references to Appendices
MAINTENAY	21.10.16		The Regiment paraded at 9 am and marched to its billeting area. HQ to CAMPAGNEUILLES-LES-GRANDES. A'Sqn. to RANG DU FLIERS. B Sqn. to AIRON-ST-VAAST - D.C. Sqn. to AIRON-NOTRE-DAME.	HQ.
CAMPAGNEUILLES LES-GRANDES.	22.10.16		Two O.R. and 2 riding horses joined from Base Rouen.	HQ.
"	23.10.16		Billets.	HQ.
"	24.10.16		Improving billets and horse standings.	HQ.
"	25.10.16		Major G.T.C. Hans. Lieut. F.G. Karinakis joined from Base.	HQ.
"	26.10.16		Lieut. C. Cantrell and 6 O.R. proceeded to MONTREUIL to unload building material for billets and stables. Improving billets.	HQ.
"	27.10.16		A working party under Lieut. C. Kalinakis proceeded to AIRON-NOTRE-DAME to dig and load chalk for Divisional School at MERLIMONT PLAGE.	HQ.
"	28.10.16		Routine in billets.	HQ.
"	29.10.16		Lieut. Kalinakis to Hospital.	HQ.
"	30.10.16		Two years since the Regt. landed in France. but in Oct. 1914 attacked with guns out & officers 1 man, at present serving with Regt.	HQ.
"	31.10.16		6 O.R. joined from Rouen.	HQ.

M.A.Quinshaw
Lieut. 1 Col.
3rd Dragoon Guards.

3RD DRAGOON GUARDS

Nominal roll of all Officers, W.O's, N.C.O's and men serving with the regiment on the 31-10-16, who came to France with the regiment in October 1914.

6-11-16

Alfred Bulkeley Lt. Col.
Comdg 3rd Dragoon Gds

"Regtl. Headquarters". 3rd Dragoon Gds

Regtl No	Rank	Name	Remarks
	Lieut	H.A. Grimshaw. M.C	Eng. 16/3/15 Rejoined 2/12/15
	2/Lieut	C.E. Cordwell	
	Hon Lt.	J. Donald.	
3777	R.S.M.	B. Buxton. M.C	
5471	S.Q.M.S	Young. A	
4263	F.Q.M.S.	Logan. R	
3933	S.S.S.	Stockdale. C	
4160	S.Tptr.	Swallows. H	Eng. 9/11/14. Rejoined 2/9/15
4338	Sgt	Beesley. C	
4469	-/-	Johnson. G	
4203	-/-	Plucastle. J	
5649	-/-	Nicholls. H	
1606	-/-	Faires. T	
3896	Cpl	Strange. S	
279	L/Cpl	Rich. W	
2839	-/-	Graham. A	
3485	-/-	Lane. F	
2190	-/-	Smith. J	Eng. 27/11/14 Rejoined 12/6/16
5694	-/-	Anstey. T	
5339	-/-	Woods. G	
6606	Pte	Buttle. S	
2349	-/-	Burge. W	
5566	-/-	Butler. E	
4504	-/-	Godsman. W	Eng. 17/5/5. Rejoined.
4868	-/-	Griggs. W	
4419	-/-	Jackson. P	
257	-/-	Jones. G	
5498	-/-	Jones. T	
4513	-/-	McLellan. M	
6390	-/-	Massom. L	
5308	-/-	Mitcham. T	Eng. 23/11/14. Rejoined 11-12-15.
2342	-/-	Newton. J	
4362	-/-	Porter. S	
1770	-/-	Pinner. S	
2348	-/-	Scroggs. W	
2689	-/-	Schultz. E	Eng. 6/6/15. Rejoined
2275	-/-	Sullivan. W	Eng. 29/1/15 Rejoined 19-6-15.
2062	-/-	Thorburn. J	

"H.Qtrs" (Cont'd)

Regtl No	Rank	Name	Remarks
5696	Pte	Redman	
2897	-"-	Vincent W.	
5702	-"-	Whittall E	
5565	-"-	Wilkinson J.	
8233	-"-	Wright H.	Eng. 8/11/14. Rejoined 12/6/15.
4580	-"-	Wheeler T	

Total. H. Qtrs   3. Offrs
                     41. O.Rks.

"A" Squadron. 3rd Dragoon Guards.

Regtl. No	Rank	Name	Remarks
	Capt	N.K. Worthington. M.C.	Eng. 17/12/14. Rejoined Regt. 9/3/15.
	-"-	N. McLeod More.	Eng. 24/2/15. Rejoined Regt. 8/10/16.
	Lieut	R.B. Allen.	Eng. 17/11/14. Regt. 14/3/15. Eng. 17/3/16. Rejoined. 26-8-16
	-"-	A.B.P.L. Vincent. M.C.	
4163	S.S.M.	Bailey. G	
6016	S.S.F	McIvor. C.	Eng. 15/4/14. Rejoined 9-9-15
4809	Sgt	Woolgar. H.	Eng. 6/6/15 Rejoined 21-10-15
3285	-"-	Watson. A.	
4450	-"-	Hicks. W.T.	
5877	-"-	Ashford. W.	
1733	-"-	Patterson. G.	
4810	Cpl	Larkman. G.	Eng. 29/1/15 Rejoined 12-6-15.
2249	-"-	Lobley. G	Eng. 8/4/14 Rejoined 19-6-15
5822	-"-	Hill. C.	Eng. 6/6/16 Rejoined 5-12-15
6655	-"-	Harrison. F.	
6845	-"-	Dickerson. H.J.	
4024	-"-	Alexander. W.	
1964	-"-	Smith. J.	
2212	Cpl.S.S.	McInnes. N.	
5319	L/Cpl	Head. S.	Eng. 30-9-15 Rejoined 8-10-16
5129	-"-	Wooldridge. S.	
6542	-"-	Bishop. W.F.	
4398	-"-	Batchelor. F.	Eng. 22/5/15 Rejoined 12-2-16.
7126	-"-	Rampton J	
2418	-"-	Pee J.	
8350	-"-	Kelly	Eng. 22/4/14 Rejoined 12/6/15.
5125	-"-	Fisher. H.G	Eng. 27/11/14. Rejoined. 5-12-15
5321	-"-	Stogden. E.B.	
5949	-"-Tptr	Coote. J.	
5950	Tptr	Rowe. A.	
3992	S.S.	Birch.	
7088	-"-	Picken. J.C.	
6487	Pte.	Penhallow. C.	Eng. 17/3/15 Rejoined 12-6-15

"A" Sqdn (Cont'd)

Regtl No	Rank	Name	
6420	S.S.	Adams, W.	
758	Pte	Archer W.	
6636	"	Alexander A	
6063	"	Berry G	
5609	"	Bint P.	Eng 23/11/14 Rejoined 3-9-15
5653	"	Bowler R	
1731	"	Bruce W	
2446	"	Brookfield G.	
4271	"	Brydon R	
6659	"	Bronn E.	
5414	"	Brown J	
4703	"	Burrells A	
352	"	Carr J.	
6467	"	Cooper F.	Eng 23/11/14 Rejoined 2-10-16
6902	"	Downey F	Eng 6/6/15 Rejoined 21-10-15
5921	"	Elphick T.	
4251	"	Evans W.	
7501	"	Evans W.	
4346	"	Finlay J.	Eng 3/2/14. Rejoined 12/6/15. Eng 25/8/15. Rejoined 25/7/16.
2350	"	Fisher H.	
5418	"	Friend T.	Eng 9/11/14. Rejoined 19/6/15.
6982	"	Groom J.	
2478	"	Hunter A	
7480	"	Kirby A.	
6013	"	McNeil D.	
7183	"	Meadons A.	Eng 23/11/14. Rejoined 21-10-15
1753	"	Mitchell G.	
3846	"	Morris W.	
7022	"	Newton W.	
481	"	O'Donnell W.	
2115	"	Redmond R.	
6021	"	Robertson A.	
7472	"	Ropert C.	
1475	"	Russell T.	

'A' Sqdn (contd)

Regtl No	Rank	Name		
5374	Pte.	Shaw. H		
6099	"	Shiercliffe. T.		
5291	"	Skedd. J.		
5354	"	Skinner E.		
6463	"	Smith. W.J.		
5124	"	Smith. H.	Eng. 18/5/15.	Rejoined 21-10-15
5736	"	Tooker D.H.		
6465	"	Uzzle. J.	Eng. 12/6/15.	Rejoined 5-12-15
5657	"	Valentine. J.		
5332	"	Wild. W.E.	Eng. 8/11/14.	Rejoined. 11/3/16.
2766	"	Watson. A.C.	Eng. 8/11/14	Rejoined 12/6/16

'A' Sqdn:- Total. 4 Offs.
  74. O.Rks

"B" Squadron. 3rd Dragoon Guards

Regtl No	Rank	Name	Remarks
	Capt	C.E.R. Holroyd-Smyth. M.C	
	Lieut	C.H. Newton-Deakin	
4104	S.S.M.	Jenkins	
4330	SQMS.	Wensley	
5834	Sgt	Flutter	Eng. 6-10-15 Rejoined 19-3-16
4802	-,-	Stanley	
1875	S.S.F.	Macreadie	
5306	L/Sgt	Cox	
4799	Cpl	Voss	
4304	"	Green	Eng. 17/11/14. Rejoined 18-9-15
2368	"	Johnson	Eng. 23/11/14 Rejoined 27-8-16
698~		King	
4878	S.S.Cpl	Cooper	
5372	SaddCpl	Pass	
6314	L/Cpl	Baker	
4211	-,-	Cheverton	
6462	-,-	Hanks	
5589	-,-	Hedgecott	Eng. ~~~ Rejoined 12/5/15
2314	-,-	Jackson	
4333	-,-	Kerr	
483	Tptr	Foley	
2410	S.S.	Richardson	
5668	-,-	Gibson	Eng. 17/11/14 Rejoined 11-3-16
6562	Pte	Annetts	
4013	-,-	Anthony	
812	-,-	Ball	
1751	-,-	Barnes	Eng. 5-6-15 Rejoined 19-3-16
6416	-,-	Bettridge	
4394	-,-	Beach	
6706	-,-	Benson	
1949	-,-	Burnett	
816	-,-	Capstick	
4325	-,-	Cunningham	
880	-,-	Carter	

'B' SQDN. (Cont'd)

REGTL NO	RANK	NAME	REMARKS
5444	Pte	Comer.	
2376	-"-	Coventry	
6389	-"-	Donaldson.	
1937	-"-	Dunne	
2412	-"-	Eddy.	
5723	-"-	Goatley.	Eng. 1-10-15 Rejoined 2-10-16.
2539	-"-	Green	
2857	-"-	Harvey.	
6275	-"-	Henry	Eng. 16/2/15. Rejoined 12-6-15.
5419	-"-	Houlton.	
5401	-"-	Kerr.	
3131	-"-	Leitch.	
6054	-"-	Marshall	
6018	-"-	Martin.	
4454	-"-	McCullock	Eng 24/6/15. Rejoined 11/12/15.
5613	-"-	Merrick	
5100	-"-	Miller.	Eng. 17/11/14. Rejoined 18-9-15
2565	-"-	McCauley	
1863	-"-	Mowatt.	
3021	-"-	Querns	Eng. 13/2/15. Rejoined 17-3-16 from 6th D.Cos.
4403	-"-	Simmons	
844	-"-	Smith	
5344	-"-	Smith	
4452	-"-	Standing.	
6369	-"-	Stanley	
4919	-"-	Thompson.	
6997	-"-	Timms.	Eng. 11/2/14. Rejoined 12-6-15
2338	-"-	Voss.	
6337	-"-	Watts	
1874	-"-	Wilkinson.	
5636	-"-	Young.	
4755	-"-	Townsend	
2066	-"-	Gibbons.	Eng 6/4/5 Rejoined 26/8/16.
5132	-"-	Jullyott	Eng 29/12/14. Rejoined 16-4-16

TOTAL 'B' Sqdn. 2. Offrs
                 66 O.Rks

"C" Squadron   3rd Dragoon Gds

Regtl No	Rank	Name	Remarks
	Capt	D.E.C. Carnegy	
	-"-	H.P. Holt	
	Lieut	G.K. Benton	
4062	S.S.M.	Crane W.H.	
4050	Sgt	Gaylor S.	
5761	-"-	Hurt J	Eng. 30-9-15 Rejoined 19-3-16
1304	-"-	Johnson J.R.	
2530	-"-	Doig J.	
4484	-"-	Lardner J	Eng. 20-5-16 Rejoined 17-9-16
5524	-"-	Thewlis F	
1966	L/Sgt	Webber H	Eng. 3/4/15 Rejoined 20-6-16
3202	●	Gardner J	Eng. 28/7/15 Rejoined 13-8-16
1642	Cpl	Ash L	Eng. 22/5/16 Rejoined 17-9-16
1237	-"-	Garniss J	
5340	-"-	McKnight J.	Eng 16/11/14 Rejoined 18-6-15
1782	Fm Sgt	Wills G	
5731	Cpl	Cavill F	Eng 15/11/14 Rejoined 19-6-15
4103	-"-	Long A	
2455	●	Joss W	
2993	-"-	Barnes J	
1714	Cpl S.S	Glancey J	
6264	Sadd Cpl	Graves W	
1263	L/Cpl	Fisher J	Eng 17/5/15 Rejoined 21-10-15
6258	-"-	Brooks G	
4226	-"-	Dillon R	Eng. 23/11/14 Rejoined 5-12-16
3032	S.S	McFarlane J	
2231	-"-	Mullis A	
4011	-"-	Fairburn C	Eng. 9/4/15 Rejoined 11/3/16
5857	Tptr	Shubrook E	
4281	Pte	Allen W	Eng. 24/5/16 Rejoined 19-3-16
3985	"	Brooks F	
2630	"	Bridle H	
4296	"	Clark P	
5625	"	Coxhead C.F	
7009	L/Cpl	Davidson A	

Regtl No	Rank	Name	Remarks
4401	Pte	Dispain. F.	Eng 19-11-14 Rejoined 26-2-16
3034	-,-	Docherty. J.	Eng 10-6-15 Rejoined 5-12-16
6393	-,-	Edwards G.	Eng 9-11-14 Rejoined 5-12-16
1752	-,-	Glazier. A.	
7443	-,-	Glieg T.	Eng. 22-11-14 Rejoined 20-5-16
6312	-,-	Griffiths H	
2877	-,-	Hawkins F. W.	Eng 17-11-16
7212	-,-	Hill. W.	
6662	-,-	Hodges. W. C.	
7210	-,-	Horrocks. J.	Eng 22/11/14. Rejoined. 5-12-16
2580	-,-	Howieson. W.	
2540	-,-	Ivemy. A	
2400	-,-	Jones. J.	Eng 31/12/14 Rejoined 12-6-15.
6494	-,-	King. J.	
4927	-,-	King W.	
6721	-,-	Lennane F	
2375	-,-	Litchfield. R.	Eng 3-10-15 Rejoined 11-6-16
4425	-,-	Lyford. A	
6573	-,-	McKay. J.	
5697	-,-	Nicholls. E	
5271	-,-	Packham H	
2390	-,-	Parfitt G.	Eng 23-2-15 Rejoined 7-11-15.
2332	-,-	Park M.	
787	-,-	Parmley R	Eng. -/4/14 Rejoined /5/15.
6769	-,-	Penny. R	Eng 17-5-15 Rejoined. 16-4-16
5469	-,-	Reffell. J.	Eng Rejoined 6-6-15
4384	-,-	Robinson. H	Eng. 9-11-14. Rejoined 12-6-15
4250	-,-	Robb J	
6346	-,-	Rollaston. T.	
5296	-,-	Rumney. J.	
6831	-,-	Scott. J.	Eng 13-11-14 Rejoined 27-8-16
4355	-,-	Simkins. B.	
4192	-,-	Somerville. F.	Eng. 17-5-15 Rejoined 27-2-16
6519	-,-	Stephenson. A.	
6401	-,-	Stephens W.	
6858	-,-	Williams. W.	Eng. 9-11-14 Rejoined 16-6-16

C' Sqdn Total. 3. Offs 68 O.Rks

WAR DIARY
INTELLIGENCE SUMMARY.
(Erase heading not required.)

Army Form C. 2118.

3rd D.G'ds   Vol 22

Place	Date	Hour	Summary of Events and Information	Remarks and references to Appendices
BLACK SANDS	1-11-16		Improvement of billets and winter accommodation was seen to by Squadrons.	M.C.
	2-11-16		Routine in billets	M.C.
	3-11-16		—	M.C.
	4-11-16		—	M.C.
	5-11-16	10.30a	Divine Service was held at AIRON-ST-VAAST	M.C.
	6-11-16		Winter Training Commenced. Sqdn and Regimental Drill	M.C.
	7-11-16		Capt J.F.C. CARNEGY, Capt. N.K. NORTHINGTON M.C. Capt C.F.R HOLROYD-SMITH M.C. and 6 Servants reported to the Agt. Divnl Training School for Course of instruction for 2 weeks. A Grooming party of 1 N.C.O and 6 men were attached to the 3rd Fld Sqdn R.E's	M.C.
	8-11-16		Winter Training	M.C.
	9-11-16		—	M.C.
	10-11-16		— Lieut. R.B. ALLEN attached to the LA M.G. Sqdn for training.	M.C.
	11-11-16		Reinforcement of 6 O.Rks, 1 Light Draught, 9 Riding Horses and	M.C.
	12-11-16		9 Chargers arrived from ROUEN. Divine Service was held at AIRON-ST-VAAST	M.C.
	13-11-16		Winter Training was continued. No A106 R.S.M. H.F+ G. BIRTLES A died	M.C.

WAR DIARY
INTELLIGENCE SUMMARY

Army Form C. 2118.

Place	Date	Hour	Summary of Events and Information	Remarks and references to Appendices
	14/1/16		Winter Training	A/c
	15/1/16		The funeral of S.S.M.F.G. Birtles took place at Etaples Cemetery. All Senior N.C.O's attended and 1 Officer per Sqdn.	A/c
	16/1/16		Winter Training	A/c
	17/1/16		Major I.T. Cliff proceeded to the Cav. Corps. H.Q. to undergo a course of instruction in the duties of Regimental Intelligence Officer.	A/c
	18/1/16		Regimental Tactical Exercise. Divine Service was held at AIRON-ST-VAAST. All Squadron Leaders rejoined from the Divisional School.	A/c
	19/1/16			A/c
	20/1/16		Winter Training continued. 2/Lieut G. Briggs, proceeded to England to report to the Indian Office to transfer to the Indian Cavalry. 2/Lieut M.H. Dulson proceeded to the Anti-Gas School for course of instruction.	A/c
	21/1/16		Winter Training. Capt N. McLeod More, Lieut W.G. Bagnall and 2/Lieut L. Helmer proceeded to the Divnl School for 4 weeks course of instruction.	A/c
	22/1/16		Winter Training. Lieut Hon V.A. Bruce. 11th Hussars was attached to the regiment for 10 days training and posted to "A" Sqdn. 2/Lieut M.H. Dulson rejoined from Gas School.	A/c

WAR DIARY
— or —
INTELLIGENCE SUMMARY.
(Erase heading not required.)

Army Form C. 2118.

Instructions regarding War Diaries and Intelligence Summaries are contained in F. S. Regs., Part II. and the Staff Manual respectively. Title pages will be prepared in manuscript.

Place	Date	Hour	Summary of Events and Information	Remarks and references to Appendices
	82/7/16		Winter Training	A.C. G.R.
	84/7/16		— " —	A.C.
	85/7/16		Regimental Tactical Scheme. Reinforcement of A Riding Horse joined from Rouen.	
	86/7/16		Maj.-Gen. Vaughan C.B., D.S.O., Comdg 3rd Cavalry Division inspected the billets of 'A' and 'B' Sqns and expressed himself satisfied with what he had seen. No 1304 Sgt. T. R. Johnson proceeded to Anti-Gas School to course of instruction.	A.C.
Berck Sands	87/7/16		The regiment carried out Sqdn and Regimental Drill on the sands at Berck. 2/Lieut D. A. S. Fitz-R. Cole, and 8 other Ranks joined from Rouen. Lieuts G. K. Bentonard R. B. Allen were promoted Captain to date from 3rd July 1916. 2/Lieut M. T. Clery was Lieut 4th April 1916, N. Black 2nd July 1916.	A.C.
Bois de Verton	85/7/16		Squadron carried out practice in Trench Crossing and Tactical Exercise	A.C.
	89/7/16		Lieut Col. A. Burt, proceeded to England to take over Temporary Command of the 3rd Reserve Regiment of Cavalry for a period of 3½ months. Majr. G. T. Cliff assumed Temporary Command of the Regt.	A.C.
Berck	30/7/16		Regimental and Squadron Drill was carried out on the Sands at Berck	A.C.

Maj.
Comdg. 3rd Dragoon Gds.

Vol 23

W A R D I A R Y. December, 1916.

3rd Dragoon Guards.

Army Form C. 2118.

WAR DIARY
INTELLIGENCE SUMMARY.
(Erase heading not required.)

Instructions regarding War Diaries and Intelligence Summaries are contained in F.S. Regs., Part II. and the Staff Manual respectively. Title pages will be prepared in manuscript.

3rd Dragoon Guards
for December 1916

Place	Date	Hour	Summary of Events and Information	Remarks and references to Appendices
CAMPIGNEULLES	1/12/16		No 1304 Sgt T.R. JOHNSON rejoined from the Anti-Gas School	JAC
LES-GRANDES	2/12/16		The Regiment carried out winter training	JAC
	3/12/16		Regtl Tour for Officers and N.C.Os in the vicinity of ST JOSSE. All specialists carried out training in billets. Divine Service was held. Lieut M.J. CLERY appointed F/Adjt vice Lieut A.A. GRIMSHAW M.C. sick in England.	JAC
	4/12/16		Routine in Billets	JAC
	5/12/16		Lieut Hon V.A. BRUCE, 11th Hussars who had been attached for training proceeded to England to rejoin the Cavalry Cadet Sqdn at NETHERAVON	JAC
	6/12/16		The regiment carried out winter training. Winter Training. Lieut A.B.P.L. VINCENT. M.C. proceeded to Anti-Gas School for course of instruction.	JAC
	7/12/16		Winter Training. 2/Lieut B.H. OSMASTON. re-joined from ROUEN	JAC
	8/12/16		—	
	9/12/16		—	JAC
	10/12/16		Divine Service was held. Lieut A.B.P.L. VINCENT. M.C. rejoined from Anti-Gas School. No 5834 Sgt FLUTTER F. proceeded to Anti-Gas School	JAC

Army Form C. 2118.

3rd Dragoon Guards
for December 1916

WAR DIARY
INTELLIGENCE SUMMARY.
(Erase heading not required.)

Instructions regarding War Diaries and Intelligence Summaries are contained in F.S. Regs., Part II. and the Staff Manual respectively. Title pages will be prepared in manuscript.

Place	Date	Hour	Summary of Events and Information	Remarks and references to Appendices
	1/12/16		Winter Training. Lieut N. Black, 2/Lieut V. Oakley Brown and 4. Other Ranks joined from Rouen.	JC
	12/12/16		Winter Training. No 4546 RQMS Harwood H. proceeded to Havre Depôt for a permanent Commission in the R.F.A.	JC
	13/12/16	10.15 am	A horse casting parade was held by the D.A.D.R. Cav. Corps at Airon-Notre-Dame, when 6 horses were Cast	JC
	14/12/16		Winter Training. Lieut H.A. Grimshaw M.C. struck off strength of regiment	JC
	15/12/16		No 5534 Sgt Flutter F. rejoined from Anti-Gas School. The following appeared in the London Gazette, dated Dec 10th. Temp 2/Lieuts (attd) to be Temporary Lieuts; L. Heller, E.S.B. Rhodes, C.R. Longbotham (Feb 29th).	JC
	16/12/16		Lieut A.B.P.L. Vincent M.C. proceeded to the 8th Pioneer Battalion to take over from the 3.D.G'ds (Pioneer) Company. Capt C.K. Benton, struck off strength of regiment.	JC
	17/12/16		Lieut W. Black proceeded to Anti-Gas School. Lieut C.E. Cordwell admitted hospital Lieut T. Kohler joined from the Base. Divine Service was held.	JC
	18/12/16	9 am	An inspection of the 3.D.Gds (Pioneer) Company was held by the G.O.C. at Airon-St-Vaast. Capt N. McL. Moore with 9 recruits rejoined from the Divnl School to take over command of the 3.D.Gds (Pioneer) Company.	JC

Army Form C. 2118.

3rd Dragoon Guards
for December 1916

WAR DIARY
INTELLIGENCE SUMMARY.
(Erase heading not required.)

Instructions regarding War Diaries and Intelligence Summaries are contained in F. S. Regs., Part II. and the Staff Manual respectively. Title pages will be prepared in manuscript.

Place	Date	Hour	Summary of Events and Information	Remarks and references to Appendices
	19/12/16		Lieut. W.G. Bagnell, Lieut L. Hellyer and 6 other ranks joined from the Divn Depot.	H/c
Airon-St-Vaast	20/12/16	1·30 pm	Capt. K. McL. More, Lieuts G.R.P. Alsop, 2/Lieuts R.D. Younger, M.V.T. Mott, D.A.S. Fitz-R. Cole, V. Oakley Brown, 863 Other Ranks, 82 Light Draught Horses, 3 L.G.S. Wagons, 1 mallier Cart and 1 watr-cart proceeded to MARESQUEL to entrain with a view to relieving the 8th Gunners Battalion.	H/c
			Capt. R.B. Allen and 2 Servants rejoined from L" M.G. Sqdn. 2/Lieut G.S.F. Tenison, rejoined sick in England.	H/c H/c
	22/12/16		The regiment made preparations for the inter-change of billets with R.H. Gds.	
	23/12/16		The regiment proceeded at CAMPIGNEULLES-LES-GRANDES at 11·15 am and marched to the new billeting area, arriving at about 3 pm "A" Sqdn to MARLES, H.Q.'s "B" Sqdn to AIX-EN-ISSART, "C" Sqdn to MARENLA.	H/c H/c H/c
	24/12/16		The regiment settled down in new billets. Capt H.P. Holt struck off strength of regiment. Divine Service was held at MARANT.	H/c H/c
	25/12/16		XMAS DAY. 2/Lieut B.H. Osmaston, reported sick in England. Routine in billets.	H/c H/c
	26/12/16			
	27/12/16		Lieut N. Black, admitted to hospital. No 5997 Sgt Shannon H. Instructed to Anti-Gas School	H/c

Army Form C. 2118.

3rd Dragoon Guards
for December 1916

WAR DIARY
INTELLIGENCE SUMMARY.
(Erase heading not required.)

Instructions regarding War Diaries and Intelligence Summaries are contained in F. S. Regs., Part II. and the Staff Manual respectively. Title pages will be prepared in manuscript.

Place	Date	Hour	Summary of Events and Information	Remarks and references to Appendices
	28/12/16		Lieut C.H. NEWTON-DEAKIN, Lieut T. KOHLER, 2/Lieut L.F. BOWATER, 2/Lieut M.H. DIXON and 9 other ranks proceeded to the Divnl School.	Allii
	29/12/16		Routine in billets	K.F.C.
	30/12/16	10:30am	The A.D.V.S. 2nd Cav Divn inspected the horses of 'B' Sqn	K.F.C.
		2pm	" " " " " 'C' "	
	30/12/16 31/12/16		Routine in billets. The V.O. inspected the horses of H.Q. Sqn at 2.30pm Divine Service was held.	K. K.
	31/12/16			

Alex
Major
Comdg. 3rd Dragoon Gds

WAR DIARY or INTELLIGENCE SUMMARY

Army Form C. 2118.

3rd Dragoon Guards
Vol 24

Place	Date	Hour	Summary of Events and Information	Remarks and references to Appendices
AIX-EN-ISSART	1917			
	1-1-19		Improvement of Billets	WAG
	2		" " "	WAG
	3		A Cinematograph entertainment in the evening.	WAG
	4		Routine in billets.	WAG
	5		P. A.D.V.S. inspected the "C" Sqdn horses.	WAG
	6		2/Lieut. G.S.F. Tenison Struck off the Strength.	WAG
	7		Divine Service	WAG
	8		Lieut. H.A. Quinshun joined from England. 4 O.R. joined from Rouen	WAG
	9		Inspection of Transport by O.C. ASC.	WAG
	10		2/Lieut. C.E. Condrick Struck off Strength.	WAG
	11		Routine in Billets	WAG
	12		2/Lieut. T.A.S. Cole rejoined from 6 Pioneer Batt"	WAG
	13		Routine in Billets.	WAG
	14		6 O.R joined from Rouen. 2/Lieuts. R.D. Younger and 2/Lieut. V. Ocheley - Brown joined from 6. P.B.M.G.	WAG
	15		2/Lieut. D.A.S. Cole & Pte. PORTER to Div. Sig. Sch"!	WAG
	16		Routine in Billets	WAG

Army Form C. 2118.

3rd Dragoon Guards

WAR DIARY
or
INTELLIGENCE SUMMARY.
(Erase heading not required.)

Instructions regarding War Diaries and Intelligence Summaries are contained in F.S. Regs., Part II and the Staff Manual respectively. Title pages will be prepared in manuscript.

Place	Date	Hour	Summary of Events and Information	Remarks and references to Appendices
AIX EN ISSART	17.		Routine in Billets.	MM9.
"	18.		" - " - "	MM9.
"	19.		Lieut-Colonel A. Burt rejoins from England.	MM9.
"	20.		Improvement of Billets.	MM9.
"	21.		" - " - "	MM9.
"	22.		2/Lieut. J.T. Thompson and 3 O.R. joined from Rouen.	MM9.
"	23.		Lieut W. Black joined from hospital	MM9.
"	24.		Improvement of Billets.	MM9.
"	25.		" - " - "	MM9.
"	26.		" - " - "	MM9.
"	27.		Lieut C.H. Newton-Deakin, 2/Lt. T. Kohler, 2/Lt L.F. Bowater & 2/Lt. M.H. Dubois Y.P.O.A.	MM9.
"	28.		rejoined from Div. School.	MM9.
"	29.		Improvement of Billets.	MM9.
"	30.		" - " - "	MM9.
"	31.		Lieut G.R.P. Abbop, 2/Lt G.W. Whittall, 2/Lt R.D. Younger and 2/Lt V. Carey Brown to Div. School.	MM9.

M A Quinton
Lieut & Ad.,
3" Dragoon Guards.

3RD DRAGOON GDS
WAR DIARY
INTELLIGENCE SUMMARY

Army Form C. 2118.

Vol 25

Place	Date	Hour	Summary of Events and Information	Remarks and references to Appendices
AIX-EN-ISSART	1.2.17		Routine in Billets.	WAQ.
	2.		Improvement of Billets.	WAQ.
	3.		2/Lieut. J.F. Thompson rejoined from Anti-Gas School.	WAQ.
	4.		2/Lieut. D.A.S. FitzRoy Cole & 1.O.R. Jones from Div. Sig. School.	WAQ
	5.		Lieut. and Qrm. J. Donald proceeded to Pioneer Batt.	WAQ
	6.		Commanding Officer inspects 'C' Sqdn Saddlery.	WAQ.
	7.		" " " " " 'B' " "	WAQ.
	8.		" " " " " 'A' " "	WAQ.
	9.			WAQ.
	10.		Routine in billets.	WAQ.
	11.		" " "	WAQ
	12.		" " "	WAQ
	13.		All officers in the Regt met the Commanding Officer on Hill 85 (MARANT) at 2:30 pm and carried out a staff ride.	WAQ
	14.		Commanding Officer and V.O. inspects 'A' Sqdn Horses.	WAQ.
	15.		Inspection of 'B' Sqdn Horses. 2/Lieut. J. Thompson and 2/Lieut. D.A.S. Cole & 2 Servants proceed to WARLUS for attachment to 12 Inf. Division.	WAQ. WAQ-

Army Form C. 2118.

WAR DIARY
INTELLIGENCE SUMMARY.
(Erase heading not required.)

Place	Date	Hour	Summary of Events and Information	Remarks and references to Appendices
AIX-EN-ISSART	16		Inspection of "C" Sqdn. Horses by Commanding Officer.	WAR 9.
	17.		Lieut-Col. A. Burt presented to TALNAS to be presented with the Légion d'honneur (Croix d'officer) by General Nivelle.	WAR 9.
	18.		2/Lieut. N. Black, 2/Lieut. T. Kohler, 2/Lieut. A.H. Dulson joined the Cav. Pioneer Batt. 5993 Sgt Andrews proceeds to Allies Gas.	WAR 9.
	19.		2/Lieut. M.I. Cleary proceeded to Cavalry Corps Signals for Course.	WAR 9.
	20.		Routine in Billets.	
	21.		All Regt Signallers were inspected by the O.C. 3 Signal Sqdn. who expressed his satisfaction at their work.	WAR 9.
	22.		The Commanding Officer held a Tactical Tour in all Officers. Capts Pearo, I. Bower, E. O'Skerman, J.P. Ball, swen have joined from Rouen.	WAR 9. WAR 9. WAR 9. WAR 9. WAR 9.
	23.		— — —	
	24.		Routine in Billets.	
	25.		Commanding Officer attended Gas School.	WAR 9.
	26.		Seven O.R. joined from Rouen.	WAR 9.
	27.		Routine in Billets.	WAR 9.
	28.			WAR 9.

M.A. Grimshaw.
Lieur (A)i
3rd Dragoon Guards.

Army Form C. 2118.

WAR DIARY
INTELLIGENCE SUMMARY. — 3ʳᵈ DRAGOON GDS
(Erase heading not required.)

Place	Date	Hour	Summary of Events and Information	Remarks and references to Appendices
AIX-EN-ISSART.	1.3.17		Routine in Billets.	B.H.O.
	2.3.17		"	B.H.O.
	3.3.17		"	B.H.O.
			Capt. G.R.C. Twistleton-Wykeham-Fiennes, Lieut M.R.Pm.Vincent,M.C; 2ⁿᵈ Lieut; B.H. Osmaston; 2/Lt J.F. Thompson, 2/Lt. J.P. Brill and 9 O.R. to Divisional Training School.	B.H.O.
	4.3.17		2/Lieut J. Whiffs and 3 O.R. arrived from ROUEN.	B.H.O.
	5.3.17		Inspection of horses by G.O.C.	B.H.O.
	6.3.17		Routine in Billets.	B.H.O.
	7.3.17		Inspection of "C" Sqdn; horses by G.O.C.	B.H.O.
	8.3.17		Routine in Billets.	B.H.O.
	9.3.17		Inspection of "C" Sqdn; horses by G.O.C.	B.H.O.
	10.3.17		Routine in Billets.	B.H.O.
	11.3.17		2/Lt C.H. Newton-Deakin + 12 other ranks attached to 3ʳᵈ Field Squadron for Cav. Pioneer Course. Inspection of R.T.C. Squadron horses by G.O.C.	B.H.O.

WAR DIARY
INTELLIGENCE SUMMARY.
(Erase heading not required.)

Army Form C. 2118.

Place	Date	Hour	Summary of Events and Information	Remarks and references to Appendices
	March 12.		Routine in Billets	B.M.O.
	13.		Inspection of "A" Sqdn: Billets by G.O.C.	B.M.O.
	14.		Inspection of "B" Sqdn: Billets by C.O. Capt: N.R. Worthington M.C. to Anti-Gas-School. Inspection of "A" Sqdn: horses by G.O.C. 2/Lieut: R.I.P. Vaughan and 2/Lieut P.A.L. Kittle and 2/Lieut: W.C. Wilkins joined from Rouen.	B.M.O.
	15.		The Pioneer Battalion of 7 officers and 254 O.R. rejoined. Inspection of "C" Sqdn Billets by C.O.	B.M.O.
	16.		Inspection of horses for casting D.A.R. Captain R.B. Allen and 2 servants transferred to "B" Sqdn:	B.M.O.
	17.		Routine in Billets	B.M.O.
	18.		" "	B.M.O.
	19.		Regt: was fitted with S.B.R.'s, the actual fitting being carried out in a gas-chamber at Aix-en-Issart by the A.D.G.O. M.C. Lt. H.A. Grimshaw was admitted to hospital with measles. Capt: H.A. Ross R.A.M.C. " " " "	B.M.O.

WAR DIARY
INTELLIGENCE SUMMARY.
(Erase heading not required.)

Army Form C. 2118.

Place	Date	Hour	Summary of Events and Information	Remarks and references to Appendices
	March 20.		Lt. M.J. Clery and 2 O.R. attached 35th Aeroplane Sqdn; for a course of Aeroplane-signalling.	Rro.
	21.		Capt: G.R.C. T-W-Fiennes M/H.; R.H. Smaslan, 2/Lt: J. P. Brill. 2/Lt: J. J. Thompson and 9 O.R. rejoined from Div: school.	Rro.
	22.		No 4799 L-Sergt Voss H. transfrd pigeon school Brigade Route March	Rro. Rro.
	23.		Lt. A.B. P.L. Vincent M.C. rejoined from Div: school.	Rro.
	24.		Divine service at MARANT at 11 A.M.	Rro.
	25.		Capt: V.E.C. Carnegy, 2/Lt: L. Bower and 40 O.R. proceeded to ARRAS as a working party.	Rro.
	26.		Routine in Billets	Rro.
	27.		2/Lt: E.A.L. Kitte and 33 O.R. proceeded to ARRAS to join the body that proceeded on 25th	Rro.
			Lt: Y.H. Grimshaw M.C. and Capt. H.A. Rome R.A.M.C. from hospital	Rro.
	28. 29. 30. 31.		Regtl (Aeroplane) Scheme Routine in Billets.	Rko. Lt. J. A. G. B.H. Amwhi

WAR DIARY
INTELLIGENCE SUMMARY

Army Form C. 2118.

3rd Dragoon Guards
April 1917

Vol 27

Place	Date	Hour	Summary of Events and Information	Remarks and references to Appendices
	1-4-17		Routine in Billets.	R.t.O.
	2-4-17		Receiving warning orders that the Bde. would move into a new area on 5th inst. — All stores — were evacuated to Dumps.	R.t.O.
	3-4-17		Regt. packed up.	R.t.O.
	4-4-17		Regt. slept in.	R.t.O.
	5-4-17.		Regt. paraded, complete with A+B echelons, at 9.35 a.m. at MARENLA, and marched to AUBEN-ST-VAAST where it went into billets at 11.15 a.m. — Reinforcements of 3.O.R. (mins'd) — The dismounted party (2/Lt. Thompson and 12.O.R.) proceeded to BEAURAINVILLE — Capt. Fiennes, Lt. Robben, 2/Lt. Wilkins + 2/Lt. Steadman proceeded to Base at ROUEN.	R.t.O.
	6-4-17		Regt. remained at AUBEN-ST-VAAST where orders were received that the forward march would be continued on the morrow.	R.t.O.
	7-4-17		The regt. paraded at 8 a.m. at AUBEN-ST-VAAST and marched to VACQUERIE-LE-BAUCQ where it went into Billets.	R.t.O.
	8/4/17 – 11/4/17		See attached typewritten account.	R.t.O.

Army Form C. 2118.

3 Dragoon Guards
April 1917

WAR DIARY
or
INTELLIGENCE SUMMARY.
(Erase heading not required.)

Instructions regarding War Diaries and Intelligence Summaries are contained in F.S. Regs., Part II. and the Staff Manual respectively. Title pages will be prepared in manuscript.

Place	Date	Hour	Summary of Events and Information	Remarks and references to Appendices
	12.4.17		Regt: paraded at RACE-COURSE, ARRAS at 9.30 a.m. and marched to FOSSEUX where it was billeted in huts.	R.T.O.
	13.4.17		Regt: remained in huts at 4 hours notice.	R.T.O.
	14.4.17		" " " " " " "	
	15.4.17		Regt: paraded at 7.45 a.m. and moved S.W. to billets at GENNE IVERGNY & TOLLENT.	R.T.O.
	16.4.17		Regt: remained in above billets.	
	17.4.17		Corps and Divisional Commanders visited the regt; and expressed their satisfaction of the work done on April 11th	R.T.O.
	18.4.17		The regt: paraded at 8.45 a.m. at TOLLENT and proceeded to new billets at GRAND-PREAUX, PETIT-PREAUX, ARGOULES and SAULCHOY.	R.T.O.
	19.4.17		Routine in billets.	
	20.4.17		" " "	} R.T.O.
	21.4.17		" " "	
	22.4.17		Divine Service was held at SAULCHOY.	

Army Form C. 2118.

3rd Dragoon Guards
April 1917

WAR DIARY
or
INTELLIGENCE SUMMARY.
(Erase heading not required.)

Place	Date	Hour	Summary of Events and Information	Remarks and references to Appendices
	23-4-17		Routine in Billets.	B.H.O.
	24-4-17		Inspection of "A" sqdn; billets by Commanding Officer.	B.H.O.
	25-4-17		Inspection of "A" sqdn; horses by Divisional Commander.	B.H.O.
	26-4-17		Inspection of B. +C. sqdn; billets by C.O.	B.H.O.
	27-4-17		Routine in Billets.	B.H.O.
	28-4-17		Divine Service was held at ARGOULES at 11. a.m.	B.H.O.
	29-4-17		Routine in billets.	
	30-4-17		121 Horses received from No 4 remount Depot BOULOGNE	B.H.O.

B.H.Smaeler Lt, 3. D. Grs.
for D.J. Ward 3rd Dragoon Guards

OPERATIONS OF 3rd DRAGOON GUARDS APRIL 5th - 11th 1917
ARRAS

Map Reference :-
ARRAS Sheet 51 B 1/40,000
TRENCH MAP 51 B S.W. 1/20,000

5th April, Thursday.   The Regiment marched from AIX - EN -
                        ISSART to concentrate with the Brigade at
                        AUBIN ST VAAST.
                        Strength :- Officers 25 Other Ranks 515.

6th April, Friday.   The Brigade remained at AUBIN ST VAAST.

7th April, Saturday.   The Brigade moved to VACQUERIE le BOUCQ.

8th April, Sunday   The Division concentrated about GOUY en
                        ARTOIS.
                        6th Cavalry Brigade being at FOSSEUX.
On this day Regiments were informed confidentially that Z Day
(day of attack) was to be at 5.30.a.m. the next morning.
All were in the best of spirits, the weather during the past
four days had been fine, the anticipatory orders for the
operation were well understood, everyone felt that they knew
what their respective duties were, and all were full of
enthusiasm.

9th April, Monday.   The Division "stood to" at one hours
                        notice, from 7.30.a.m., the attack having
been postponed to commence at that hour.
At 8.30.a.m. information was received that the German first system
of trenches in front of ARRAS had been taken and shortly after
that the order was received for the Brigade to be clear of
FOSSEUX by 12 noon.
The Division closed up on the road GOUVES - DUISANS - ARRAS
with head just W of ARRAS, for its Approach march.
At about 5.p.m. the 6th Cavalry Brigade which had advanced to
the Railway near the Cemetry E of ARRAS, but as the final
objectives MONCHY LE PREUX - LA BERGERE had not been captured the
Division went into bivouac on N.E. outskirts of the town and
late at night moved to just S of LOUEZ
During the halt near the Cemetery the Brigadiers and Commanding
Officers had gone forward to the captured German trenches just
N. of TILLOY to make a personal reconnaissance and to learn
the Cavalry track.
It was a bitterly cold, snowy night.

10th April, Tuesday.   At about 10.30.a.m. the Division moved
                        forward and went in to a "position of
readiness" N. of the CAMBRAI Road about 1,000 yards N. of
TILLOY les MAFFLAINES, where it was massed and "A" Squadron,
3rd Dragoon Guards was sent on to construct four crossings over
the WANCOURT - FEUCHY Trench line. The final objectives of the
Infantry were still not in possession of our troops.
The O.C. 3rd Dragoon Guards went forward to the FEUCHY line to
find out the situation, and patrols were sent to report on the
progress of the Infantry at LA BERGERE and MONCHY le PREUX;
2/Lieut Cole to the former (mounted) and 2/Lieut Whipp to the
latter (dismounted).
At 3.p.m. the 6th and 8th Cavalry Brigades with "C" and "G"
Batteries R.H.A. advanced to a position W of the FEUCHY line,
about 1,000 yards W. of FEUCHY CHAPEL, where they came under a
certain amount of shelling which caused a few casualties in men
and horses. the afternoon advance
At 7.p.m. having been postponed on account of a fresh attack
on MONCHY being found necessary, and it being very late, the
6th Brigade moved back to a safer position about 2,000 yards W
where it bivouaced for the night. The four crossings over the
FEUCHY trench had been completed during the afternoon of this
day.

11th April, Wednesday   At 5.30.a.m. the 3rd Dragoon Guards, 1
Section M.G. (2/Lieut Lowther) Section "G" R.H.A. (Lieut FitzPatrick) the
final position H.33.d. which had been occupied on the 10th. Officers
Patrols were continually sent out to keep touch with the Infantry at
LA BERGERE and MONCHY LE PREUX, and a permanent Patrol of 2/Lieut
Rowsher and 4 men was sent as liason with the 8th Cavalry Brigade
immediately on our left, the other Patrols were under 2/Lieut Whipp
2/Lieut Vaughan, 2/Lieut Whittall, Lieut Camaston, 2/Lieut Oakley-
Brown, 2/Lieut Dulson.
The information of these Patrols was very good and the G.O.C.,
Brigade was in continual touch with the local situation.
At 6.a.m. the 6th Cavalry Brigade Report Centre moved to H.33.d.
At 8.30.a.m. a report was received from G.O.C., 112th Infantry Brigade
that it was practically certain that MONCHY LE PREUX and LA BERGERE were
in our hands, (this may have been the case for a short time, but both
places were counter attacked and fighting was still in actual progress
in these places when we moved). On the above information being received the order
was given for the 6th and 8th Brigades to advance. A conference was
held just before the advance between Lieut Colonel Whitmore D.S.O.
O.C. Essex Yeomanry, leading Regiment of the 8th Brigade, and
Lieut Colonel A. Burt O.C. 3rd Dragoon Guards, leading Regiment of
the 6th Brigade
A liason Officer   and 4 men joined Regimental Headquarters
from Essex Yeomanry.
The leading Regiments of the 6th and 8th Brigades advanced over the
FEUCHY trenches parallel to each other.
First Bound of 3rd Dragoon Guards was to Contour 100 just North of
CAMBRAI Road 1,000 yards E of FEUCHY CHAPEL.
Order of March :- Advance Guard "B" Squadron, and M.G. Section,
Main Body Headquarters, Section R.H.A., "C" Squadron, "A" Squadron.
"B" Squadron sent forward an Officers Patrol to the Sunken Road South
of MONCHY LE PREUX immediately the order to advance was received.
Slight shelling was experienced in moving to the first bound, on
reaching which "B" Squadron and M.G. Section under Captain Holroyd -
Smyth M.C. moved straight on to first objective (Ridge South of
MONCHY) with No 1 (Lieut Dulson's) Troop extended in advance,
remainder of Squadron followed in line of troop columns. The rest
of the Regiment formed up by Squadrons in line of troop columns with
Section R.H.A. echeloned behind "A" under cover of Ridge Contour 100.
The O.C. 3rd Dragoon Guards and Adjutant (Lieut H.A.Grimshaw M.C.),
with O.C. Section R.H.A. moved to a position of observation.
As "B" Squadron reached spur running South of MONCHY LE PREUX "C"
Squadron (Major Cliff) advanced in line of troop columns and galloped
steadily to the right of "B" Squadron, followed on their arrival by
the O.C. 3rd Dragoon Guards, Adjutant, and O.C. Section R.H.A. with
1 Troop "A" Squadron, remainder of "A" Squadron and Section R.H.A.
under Captain Worthington M.C. following 500 yards behind.
Brigade Headquarters and remainder of 6th Cavalry Brigade moved up
to position left by 3rd Dragoon Guards at Contour 100, where it
remained in Reserve.

The Advance of "B" Squadron
Heavy shelling was experienced immediately after leaving Contour 100
and 3 German Machine Guns continually swept the Valley between
FEUCHY CHAPEL and LA BERGERE causing a good many casualties among
the horses.
At about 9.5.a.m. the leading troop reached the MONCHY LE PREUX -
LA BERGERE Road at South exit of MONCHY VILLAGE where it dismounted
and took up a fire position along the road O.1.c.3.o. to O.1.c.3.3.
On halting No 1 Troop came under heavy shell and M.G. fire. The
Squadron arrived immediately afterwards, left troop No 4 supporting
No 1 about the same position, the centre troop No 3 with the
Squadron Leader took up a position in H.12.b.2.7. and the right troop
No 2, in H.12.b.6.6. just South of Nos 1 and 4.
On its arrival the Squadron came under heavy shell and M.G. fire
and suffered a good many casualties, amongst the killed were
Lieut C.H.Newton Deakin, Sergts Flutter and Stanley, Corpl King and
Pte Hoy. 2/Lieut M.H.Dulson was wounded.

(3)

The front of the Squadron was swept by hostile Artillery barrage and very heavy M.G. fire.
Germans were seen advancing in strength from the N.E. at O.2.a. and from BOIS DES AUBEPINES, and a general movement from ST ROHARTS FACTORY towards BOIS DU VERT was observed.
Hotchkiss Rifles and Machine Guns were turned on to the enemy and in co-operation with the Essex Yeomanry the enemy's effort was effectually stopped.
At 9.20.a.m. "C" Squadron arrived and took up a position from Pt 95. 58. in N.12.b. to N.12.b.7.7. with Hotchkiss Rifle posts pushed forward to Road LA BERGERE - MONCHY LE PREUX, joining with "B" Squadron on the left and the advance Infantry (about 50 men N.Lancs) at LA BERGERE on the right, an observation post being pushed out to the East of the Windmill just North of this place.
The Squadron occupied a line in a half moon shape in a German trench which had just been started and on which work was immediately begun, continued by our men
On dismounting the Squadron came under heavy shell and M.G. fire, Sergt Garniss was killed and several men wounded. Hotchkiss Rifles immediately came into action against the German movement about O.8.central and on the CAMBRAI Road at O.14.a. with good effect.
Patrols were sent from "B" and "C" Squadrons to the bank in O.7.a. and c. and the valley about O.7.b. and d.
On "C" Squadron reaching its position North of LA BERGERE, O.C., 3rd Dragoon Guards, Adjutant, and O.C. Section R.H.A., with 1 troop "A" Squadron galloped forward to a position about 300 yards N.E. of LES FOSSES FARM about N.12.a.4.8. followed shortly afterwards by the rest of "A" Squadron and Sect of R.H.A. These arrived at about 9.30.a.m.
Each party came under M.G. fire from GUEMAPPES when crossing the valley N.N.W. of LES FOSSES FARM and had a certain number of horses wounded.
The O.C. 3rd Dragoon Guards went up to see Major G.T. Cliff and to study the situation.
Communication was opened with the rear by signalling.
The Section R.H.A. took position and fired on enemy at BOIS DU VERT.
As the right flank was exposed and Germans were seen concentrating and threatening to advance from WANCOURT and GUEMAPPES, a troop and two Hotchkiss Rifles were sent from "A" Squadron to strengthen the Infantry about 20 men of different Battalions of the 112th Infantry Brigade at LES FOSSES FARM. This troop occupied a small trench just South of LES FOSSES FARM.
At about 10.15.a.m. another Section of "C" R.H.A. arrived, and Major Scarlett Commanding the Battery came up and studied the situation.
At about 12 noon orders were received from Brigade Headquarters for the guns and the horses of the Regiment to be sent back to the position of the Brigade Reserve.
This movement caused a good deal of shelling and some casualties occurred on the way back. The Regiment was however lucky in having carried this out when it did, as German aeroplanes, 5 in number, had been over the position and 10 minutes after the horses left the whole valley was heavily shelled for two hours, particularly the ground where the guns and Squadron horses had been, with a special interest in the Regimental Headquarters Shell hole.
The 8th Brigade on our left which had evidently received similar orders appeared to suffer severely in taking the horses back.
At about 2.p.m. a movement of Germans was seen going from BOIS DU VERT to ST ROHARTS FACTORY and large parties were observed collecting about 20 at a time behind the building 100 yards N.W. of that place in O.14.a. where a troop of Cavalry was also observed. A post was immediately put out from our lines to get better command of the CAMBRAI Road. A battery which could be clearly seen in action close to ST ROHARTS FACTORY was reported to Brigade Headquarters.
At about 2.30.p.m. on account of reports of the enemy massing for a counter attack and the weakening of the troops available on the spot through all No 3s going back with the led horses, the G.O.C. Brigade sent forward a Section of Machine Guns and 1 Squadron N.S.Y. (Major West) to re-inforce our line.
The counter Attack was anticipated for the following reasons :-
(1) German Infantry and Cavalry Patrols had been seen collecting about GUEMAPPES, ST ROHARTS FACTORY, and at the Woods N.E. and E

of MONCHY LE PREUX and parties had attempted to advance on our line from these places.
(2) The importance of MONCHY LE PREUX as a tactical position, which was very obvious.
(3) A battery of 4 German guns calibre about 4.2" which was abandoned and in position near Regimental Headquarters in N.12.a. also a large quantity of gun ammunition in the Artillery dug out.
(4) Preparatory Artillery and M.G. barrage which was started by the enemy.

At about 3.p.m. an attack by apparently 3 Companies of Gordon Hlrds on GUEMAPPES from half a mile S.W. of LES FOSSES FARM appeared to be brought to a standstill about 600 yards from GUEMAPPES by an intense German Artillery barrage.

At about 3.30.p.m. the N.S.Y. Squadron and M.G. Section arrived dismounted and although fatigued by a long march with all their equipment and ammunition they went off at once, full of enthusiasm, to take their place in the front line.

Two troops were attached to the front line Squadrons, and owing to the right at LA BERGERE being threatened from GUEMAPPES, and the weakness of the force at this place 2 troops and 1 M.G. Section were sent under Lieut Pope M.C. to strengthen this flank. The latter party occupied a trench South of the CAMBRAI Road where about 25 Infantry of 4 different battalions had been organised into a defence post by Pte Batchelor, 6th Bedfords. This man had collected German rifles, ammunition and bombs for his party, as his men only had 5 rounds a man left.

Major West took charge of this section of trench and re-organised the defence.

On the arrival of the Regiment in its position:-
The right ("C" Squadron) was in touch with a few details of the 112th Infantry Brigade about LA BERGERE, and the left ("B" Squadron) was in touch with the Essex Yeomanry, 8th Cavalry Brigade and a few details of the 111th Infantry Brigade at MONCHY LE PREUX, 1 troop was put into the houses at southern outskirts of the latter village next to which was an Infantry M.G. and 2 men. No ther troops had apparently been on the front of this line. A battery of 4 guns and a large quantity of ammunition had been abandoned in N.12.a. and the Germans had hastily left the trench they were preparing between LA BERGERE and MONCHY LE PREUX.

At about 5.p.m. instructions were received from Brigade Headquarters that the troops would be relieved this evening.

At about 5.45.p.m. parties of the 13th K.R.Rs. came through MONCHY LE PREUX and commenced to build strong points in front of "B" Squadron. O.C. 3rd Dragoon Guards visited the line and found all correct and in excellent order, the men had worked splendidly and the Germans had ceased to worry for the time being.

Various hostile working parties had been seen and satisfactorily dealt with.

Arrangements were made for handing over the trenches and evacuating the wounded, a collecting station being formed at LES FOSSES FARM; everything worked very smoothly.

At 11.30.p.m. the Regiment, Major West's Squadron N.S.Y., and 2 Sections 6th Machine Gun Squadron were relieved by the Sussex Regiment 36th Infantry Brigade, there was slight shelling on withdrawing but no casualties occurred.

The Regiment moved to bivouac at the Race Course Arras.

12th April, Thursday. The Brigade concentrated in huts at FOSSEUX.

ooooooooooooooooOOOooooooooooooooo

The Cavalry Corps Commander Lieut General Sir C.T.McM Kavanagh K.C.B., C.V.O., D.S.O., and the Divisional Commander Major General J. Vaughan C.B., D.S.O. visited the Regiment to express their satisfaction at the work done on the 11th April.

The casualties of the Regiment were Lieut C.M.Newton Deakin and 19 Other Ranks killed, 3 Officers and 56 Other Ranks wounded of whom 3 have died. 196 horses killed and wounded.

14/4/17 (sd) Alfred Burt Lieut Colonel
Commanding 3rd Dragoon Guards.

REPORT ON THREE SECTIONS OF 6TH MACHINE GUN SQUADRON
ATTACHED 3RD DRAGOON GUARDS ON APRIL 11th 1917.

Reference Map ARRAS Sheet 5.B 1/40?000
Trench Map 51.B. 1/20,000

At about 8.30.a.m. "B" Section (2/Lieut Lowden) moved off with "B", the advance Squadron 3rd Dragoon Guards and took up position on the right of this Squadron South of MONCHY in N.12.b., behind some manure heaps in the open.

First Target was about a dozen Germans in O.7.d. 8.4. at about 9.30.a.m.; the result was they fled leaving three on the ground. Later a party of Germans retiring in front of 8th Cavalry Brigade at 0.2.b. East of MONCHY moving South, 250 Rounds fired at range of 1000 yards; the Germans scattered.

There was a lull for about an hour and a half during which time 2/Lieut Lowden was wounded, and his Sergt (EATON) took command.

Position of Guns was changed slightly 1 Gun was placed in a shell hole and the other in a small trench behind a manure heap. Field of fire for both guns from the South edge of Hill 100, 1800 yards East of MONCHY, to ST ROHARTS FACTORY.

As belts required replenishing a man was sent to the Ammunition Dump which was with the next Squadron on the right in N.12.b. just North of LA BERGERE. Only three boxes were found remaining as the rest had been blown up.

At about 11.15.a.m. a battery of guns was reported near ST ROHARTS FACTORY and Section was asked if they could do them any damage, it was considered that the expenditure of ammunition would not be justified. Heavy artillery was put on to this Battery and shelled them with effect.

The Germans were seen running about near pt 74.11 South of BOIS DU VERT and the guns were laid on at 1700 yards with apparently good result.

For remainder of day only occasional targets were seen and the parties always dispersed on being fired on. The position was continually under Shell and Machine Gun fire which however did not get on to the places where the Machine Guns were in action.

The one man Range Finder "Barr - Stroud" worked very satidfactorily Casualties in this Section 1 Officer and 1 man wounded; 3 horses killed 2 horses wounded. 9 Belt Boxes blown up.

At about 4.30.p.m. "F" Section under Lieut Elmes followed by "E" Section under Lieut Tisdale went with Major West's Squadron N.S.Y. to reinforce 3rd Dragoon Guards just N.E. of LESS FOSSES FARM in N.12.a.

On the way "E" Section lost 2 men killed and 2 of their carrying party wounded.

"E" Section accompanied 2 Troops N.S.Y. to strengthen the right flank in a small trench immediately South of LA BERGERE in N.12.d.3.7.

30 Germans were seen trying to leave GUEMAPPES these were fired at at a range of 800 yards and dispersed. Later in the snowstorm small parties of Germans were seen near a hedge about 500 yards off towards GUEMAPPES, result of firing could not be observed owing to the snow.

The Guns were continually under fire from hostile artillery, and Machine guns especially from the direction of WANCOURT and GUEMAPPES.

Casualties 3 men Killed 2 Carriers wounded.

"F" Section had one Gun in Reserve at LA BERGERE and 1 gun in Reserve at 3rd Dragoon Guards H.Qrs North of LES FOSSES FARM. This Section had no casualties. The position was relieved at about 11.30. p.m.

2/5/17   (sd) Alfred Burt Lieut Colonel,
                  Commanding 3rd Dragoon Guards.

3rd Dragoon Guards
CASUALTIES 11th APRIL 1917

KILLED

Lieut C.H. Newton Deakin
5834 Sergt Flutter F.
4802 Sergt Stanley W.
1237 Sergt Garniss J.
6924 Corpl King W.
7009 L/Cpl Davidson A.
5770 Pte Hamilton C.
758 Pte Archer A.
5528 Pte Reeker F.
8087 Pte Bird A.
10425 Pte Hey G.
8824 Pte Payne H.
8041 Pte Pitham R.
7018 Pte Burchell H.
4685 Pte Batchelor E.
3034 Pte Docherty J.
4927 Pte King W.
7503 Pte Savage A.
6697 Pte Smith J.
2375 Pte Litchfield R. Missing believed Killed.

WOUNDED

2/Lieut D.A.S.FiteR Cole (At duty).
2/Lieut M.V.T. Mott (At duty).
2/Lieut M.H. Dulsen
2530 Sergt Deig J.
1642 L/Sergt Ash L. (Died of Wounds)
5877 Sergt Ashford W.
4504 Corpl Green J.
3285 Corpl Watson A.
4878 S.S.Cpl Cooper J.
2400 L/Cpl Jones J.
5321 L/Cpl Stegden E.
6706 L/Cpl Benson H. (At duty)
8961 L/Cpl Bird G.
12372 L/Cpl Harries A.G.
302 Pte Carr J.
7501 Pte Evans W.
4184 Pte Lardner R.
10184 Pte Roberts A.
5354 Pte Skinner E.
8170 Pte Wright W.
7408 Pte Buss G.
5124 Pte Snarey E.
10507 Pte Mitchell G.
4450 Sergt Hicks W. (At Duty)
2350 Pte Fisher W. (At Duty)
7822 Pte Davidson W. (At Duty)
5589 Pte Hedgcott E. (At Duty)
8955 S.S. Short J. (Died of Wounds)
6562 Pte Annetts C.
1957 Pte Dunne J.
6605 Pte Eaton J.
2068 Pte Gibbens J.
8066 Pte Green A.
5249 Pte Heron S.
4311 Pte Hill R
5132 Pte Julliett P. (Died of Wounds)
1184 Pte Laird J.
6018 Pte Martin L.
3114 Pte Pidduck C.
10630 Pte Cavell W.
6701 Pte Sutton G.
4452 Pte Standing J.

LIST OF CASUALTIES (continued)

WOUNDED

```
 4919 Pte Thompson J.
 7975 Pte Tickner S.
13657 Pte Smith J.
 7964 Pte Ellis L.
 1752 Pte Glazier A. (Died of Wounds)
 7953 Pte Jones J.
 7210 Pte Horrocks J.
 2540 Pte Ivsmay A.
 8658 Pte Leadbeter C.
 1838 Pte McFadden F.
 4365 Pte Simpkins B.
 5763 Pte Shellard A.
 8050 Pte Osborn J.
 9937 Pte Roberts H.S.
10429 Pte Wright H.J.
 7024 Pte Bradbury W.
 5550 Pte Wheeler F.
  481 Pte O'Donnell W.
 5124 Pte Smith
      Interpreter M.des L Castel R.
 6264 Sad Cpl Graves W.   (reported Missing, heard of in Hospital
                                    wounded)
13069 Pte Fletcher H.     ( Missing, since returned)
 6573 Pte McKay J.        ------o------
 1929 Pte Burnett H.      Missing.
```

LIST OF CASUALTIES IN DISMOUNTED PARTY

```
  845 L/Cpl Weston J.      Wounded
 5896 Pte Aldred W.C.         "
 2370 Pte Russell T.S.        "
10305 Pte Salisbury J.        "
 5314 L/Cpl Spooner E.        "
 8249 Pte Crane W.            "
 6298 Pte Cooper H.           "
 8184 Pte Sharp W.R.          "
 9824 Pte Smith F.W.          "
```

RECOMMENDATIONS FORWARDED TO BRIGADE HEADQUARTERS FOR IMMEDIATE RECOGNITION.

AT ARRAS 11th APRIL 1917.

Major Grosvenor Talbot Cliff 3rd Dragoon Guards; South of Monchy le Preux, for gallantry and good work in seizing and maintaining a position between La Bergere and Monchy le Preux under heavy shell and Machine Gun fire and for obtaining and reporting very useful and important information under great difficulties.
Germans were massing and threatening a counter attack which was stopped at the start by good fire discipline - for D.S O.

Captain Charles Holroyd Smyth M.C. 3rd Dragoon Guards, on 11th April 1917 at Arras South of Monchy le Preux, for gallantry and good work in seizing and holding a position South of and on S.E. outskirts of Monchy le Preux notwithstanding heavy shell and Machine Gun fire.
Germans were massing and threatening a counter attack which was stopped at the start by good fire discipline - for D.S.O.

Major W. West N.S.Yeo. on 11th April at Arras near La Bergere for gallantry and devotion to duty in supporting and maintaining a position South of La Bergere.
The section of line was very weakly held by some Infantry.
This Officer organised a defence and ensured the security of his position which was subjected to heavy shelling and Machine Gun fire. - for D.S.O.

No 7120 Private Rudkin E. "C" Squadron 3rd Dragoon Guards, on 11th April 1917 at Arras, South of Monchy le Preux for good work in carrying message under heavy shell and Machine Gun fire and for useful work throughout the day. - for Military Medal.

No 7819 Private Duffew, "B" Squadron, 3rd Dragoon Guards, on 11th April 1917 at arras South of Monchy le Preux for gallantry and good work in collecting and dressing wounded under heavy shell and Machine Gun fire throughout the day. - for M.Medal.

Sent through A.D.M.S. 3rd Cavalry Division
Captain Henry Albert Renn R.A.M.C. attached 3rd Dragoon Guards, on 11th April 1917 at Arras near Monchy le Preux showed gallantry and devotion to duty in dressing and collecting wounded under heavy shell fire throughout the day.
Apart from men of the Regiment this Officer was able to give assistance to Infantry and other Units in the vicinity - for M.Cross

No 13272 L/Cpl Harries A.G. "B" Squadron 3rd Dragoon Guards, on 11th April 1917 at Arras South of Monchy le Preux when sent on a message he had his right hand practically severed at the wrist but continued to try and proceed, was wounded again in the leg and crawled back to his Troop Leader to report he was unable to deliver the message. He advanced 100 yards with his arm shattered and crawled back 300 yards after being hit a second time - for V.C.

No 6494 Pte King J. "C" Squadron 3rd Dragoon Guards, on 11th April 1917 at Arras South of Monchy le Preux under heavy shell and Machine Gun fire kept touch with the Infantry on the right during the period when the situation was obscure.He obtained useful information and his position was in very open groundcontinually under fire for D.C.M.

RECOMMENDATIONS (continued)

No 13031 Private Beast F. "B" Squadron 3rd Dragoon Guards, on 11th April at Arras South of Monchy le Freux for carrying messages all day under heavy shell and machine Gun fire across the open. He was wounded in the back by a slpinter of shell about 12 noon and after his wound was dressed continued at his work and helped to improve the trench position. He has since been admitted to Hospital. - for D.C.M.

14/4/17.   (sd) Alfred Burt   Lieut Colonel.
            Commanding 3rd Dragoon Guards.

LIST OF OFFICERS PRESENT DURING OPERATIONS 5th to 11th
APRIL 1917 ABOUT MONCHY LE PREUX AND ARRAS.

Lieut Colonel A Burt   Headquarters
Lieut & Adjutant H.A. Grimshaw M.C.
Lieut M.J. Clery
Lieut B.H. Osmaston
Capt H.A. Ronn (R.A.M.C)
Capt E. Nicholsen (A.V.C.)
Lieut & Qr Mr J. Donald
2/Lieut J.P. Brill

Major G.T. Cliff   "C" Squadron
Capt N. McLeod Mere
Lieut W.G. Bagnell
Lieut W. Black
Lieut L. Hellyer
2/Lieut R.D. Younger
2/Lieut G.W. Whittall
2/Lieut M.V.T. Mott

Captain N.K. Worthington M.C. "A" Squadron
Lieut A.B.P.L. Vincent M.C.
Lieut G.R.P. Alsop
2/Lieut L.F. Bewater
2/Lieut D.A.S. FitzRoy Cole
2/Lieut J. Whipp

Captain C.E.R. Holroyd Smyth M.C. "B" Squadron
Captain R.B. Allen
Lieut C.H. Newton Deakin
2/Lieut M.H. Dulson
2/Lieut V. Oakley Brown
2/Lieut R.I.P. Vaughan

OFFICERS WITH DISMOUNTED PARTY

Captain U.E.C. Carnegy   Headquarters
2/Lieut I. Bower   "B" Squadron
2/Lieut E.A.L. Kittle   "A" Squadron

14/4/17.   Alfred Burt Lieut Colonel.
                               Commanding 3rd Dragoon Guards.

List of Honours and Rewards
   (Recent Operations)

Bar to Distinguished Service Order

Lieut Colonel A. Burt D.S.O.

Bar to Militay Cross

Lieut A.B.P.L.Vincent M.C.

Military Cross

Captain G.P.R.Alsop
Lieut M.J.Clery
Lieut G.W.Whittall

French Croix de Guerre

Captain H.A.Grimshaw M.C.

Distinguished Conduct Medal

No 19989 S.S.M.Woolgar

Military Medal

No 3202 Sergeant Gardiner J.
No 5306 Sergeant Cox C.
5340 Sergeant McKnight J.
10520 Sergeant Martin C.S.
3285 Corporal Watson A.
16571 L/Corporal Neasham F.
5539 L/Corporal Wood G.
19927 L/Corporal Seale R.
6982 L/Corporal Groom W.
2115 L/Corporal Redmond R.   D.C.M.
4013 L/Corporal Anthony B.
6659 Pte Brown E.
5489 Pte Jones F.D.
2877 Pte Hawkins F.
14666 Pte Ashby T.C.
4362 Pte Porter S.

WAR DIARY or INTELLIGENCE SUMMARY

Army Form C. 2118.

3rd Dragoon Guards

Place	Date	Hour	Summary of Events and Information	Remarks and references to Appendices
PETIT PREUX	May 1917 1		Routine in Billets. 1st Regiment, ~~Squadron~~ at this point, was refitting.	WAQ
"	2		Routine in Billets	WAQ
"	3			
"	4			
"	5			
"	6			
"	7			
"	8			
"	9			
"	10			
"	11			
"	12			WAQ
DOMPIERRE	13		1st Regiment received orders to move to a new Billeting Area, DOMPIERRE, BERTHECOURT, and moves at 9.30 a.m. Sqdns move independently.	WAQ
"	14		1st Regiment parades at VOISIN and marches to MEZEROLLES, via AUXI LE CHATEAU.	WAQ
BERTHECOURT	15		The march was resumed at 10 a.m. 1st Regiment arriving at BERTHECOURT-LES-DAMES at 5.30 pm.	WAQ
LA NEUVILLE	16		Parading at 8am 1st Regiment marches to LA NEUVILLE.	WAQ
"	17		1st Regiment remains in billets in LA NEUVILLE.	WAQ
HARBONNIÈRES	18		The fresh march was again continued, 1st Regiment arriving at HARBONNIÈRES at 12.30 p.m.	WAQ
"	19		The Regiment remains in Billets in HARBONNIÈRES.	WAQ
BUIRE	20		At 7.45 am 1st Regiment parades and marches to BUIRE, 4 miles E of PERONNE when it went into Camp. Dismd parade 13.0.R found. (Ref map 1/40,000 PERONNE) V28.a.6.5.	WAQ

WAR DIARY
or
INTELLIGENCE SUMMARY.
(Erase heading not required.)

Army Form C. 2118.

Place	Date	Hour	Summary of Events and Information	Remarks and references to Appendices
BUIRE	May 1917 21		Improvement of Camp Shelter commenced and Breastwire put up	NIL
"	22		— — —	
"	23		1/2 Regiment composed of 7 Officers and 359 O.R. Paraded at 5.30 pm and marched to EPEHY. (See Appendix)	NIL
"	24			
"	25		The Remainder, Consisting of 14 Officers and 255 O.R. Remained in Camp. 1 Man being left to 4 horses.	NIL
"	26			
"	27			
"	28			
"	29			
"	30			
"	31			

NA O Simohan. Capt.
O.C. 3rd Dragoon Gds.

WAR DIARY
or
INTELLIGENCE SUMMARY.

(Erase heading not required.)

Army Form C. 2118.

Instructions regarding War Diaries and Intelligence Summaries are contained in F. S. Regs., Part II. and the Staff Manual respectively. Title pages will be prepared in manuscript.

Place	Date	Hour	Summary of Events and Information	Remarks and references to Appendices
			Evening fine. 6th Dismounted Force H.Qrs 3rd Dragoon Guards, 7 Officers, 30 O.R. 3rd Dgn Guards, 10 Officers, 300 O.R., 1st Royal Dragoons, 10 Officers, 300 O.R., 2 R.A.M.C. attached 6th D.G. Squadron, 6 Officers, 112 O.R. took over position in GREEN LINE, billeted the night in EPEHY. 1 Officer 4 N.C.Os went to Outpost Line. 1½ Squadrons Royals took over Support line from 16th Lancers. Gas Guards taken over in EPEHY. 3rd Dragoon Guards moved to GREEN LINE. H.Qrs D.1. Sub Sector to COPSE 13. 1½ Squadrons Royals moved into Support. 1½ Squadrons to Outposts. N.S.Y. went into BROWN LINE. Weather fine. Relief complete 12.30.a.m. 25/5/17.	
			Weather fine. Casualty No 15166 Pte STRIPLING J., Royals wounded. Situation normal. Improvement to Trench line by day.	
			Weather fine. Trench Mortar fired on BIRDCAGE at 5.45.a.m. Slight shelling during the day on LITTLE PRIEL FARM. Hostile M.G. fire from OSSUS WOOD. Hostile working Party heard E.S.E of BIRDCAGE. Casualty, 1874 Pte WILKINSON D., 3rd Dragoon Guards (accidental wound). Work on Communication Trenches and deepening Fire trenches. Outpost Communication Trench improved.	
			N.S.Y. relieved Royals in Outpost & Supports. Relief completed at 3.a.m. Royals relieved 3rd Dragoon Guards in GREEN LINE. 3rd Dragoon Guards relieved N.S.Y. in BROWN LINE. Weather fine. Officers Patrol (Lieut Osmaston) 3rd Dragoon Guards went to OSSUS WOOD during the night and obtained useful Information. 2/Lieut Rice N.S.Y. reconnoitred front of BIRDCAGE 6.12.a.m. and 9.a.m. Hostile Trench Mortar fired on BIRDCAGE and ceased on our Artillery retaliation. Wiring on Outpost Line improved. Communication Trench G. & H. & J. to I improved. Casualty:- Pte DYSART.D., Royals wounded.	
			Weather fine. Our heavies shelled houses near VENDHUILLE and caused an explosion. Traffic heard on road leading through K.30. to S.19.4.2.5. Hostile Patrol advanced on Outpost Communication Trench and driven off by Hotchkiss, leaving Rifle, cap, Grenade. Casualties, No 356 Pte REID C. Royals wounded; 2314 Pte COOPER W. Royals wounded; 165498 Corporal BURNE, N.S.Y. missing.	
			Heavy rain storm. Lieut Osmaston, 3rd Dragoon Guards with 6 men entered OSSUS WOOD and found hostile wire and men talking behind it. Road shown running along N. edge of Wood found to run through centre. Trench Mortar fired on QUARRY at 6.p.m. and 11.10.p.m. Work :- Wiring of Outposts and improving Communication Trenches. Casualties :- No 155570 L/Corpl HARRIS A.V.; 165808 Pte EMERY H.; 165284 Pte Selman R.; 165541 L/Corpl WEBBER M.V.; 165432 Corpl BARRETT A.H., O.18047 165763 Pte SHEPPARD A.R.; 165376 Pte LATTERRY F.H., 165347 Pte SHALE.T., all N.S.Y. wounded	

Army Form C. 2118.

WAR DIARY
or
INTELLIGENCE SUMMARY.
(Erase heading not required.)

Instructions regarding War Diaries and Intelligence Summaries are contained in F. S. Regs., Part II. and the Staff Manual respectively. Title pages will be prepared in manuscript.

Place	Date	Hour	Summary of Events and Information	Remarks and references to Appendices
	29/3/17	10.p.m. to 1.45a.m.	3rd Dragoon Guards relieved N.S.Y. in Outpost and Support. N.S.Y. relieved Royals in GREEN LINE. Royals occupied BROWN LINE. A Patrol of the Royals went out from C. Post to VILLAGE and found trench N. & S. across TOMBOIS FARM and VENDHUILLE Road occupied. Two Salpers were located, 1 in enemy's trench line and 1 about F.5.d.3.4. Our M.Gs were active on PONTOON BRIDGE and OSSUS VILLAGE. Four parties of enemy each 20 strong seen working in direction of VENDHUILLE on road 5.28.a.1.9. Search lights seen N.E. during the night. Casualties :- No 185548 L/Corpl WATTS R.P. N.S.Y. wounded, 11057 Pte STEVENS A., 3rd Dragoon Guards Absent from Bivouac. Weather fine.	
	30/3/17		Officers Patrol, Lieut Osmaston and 2/Lieut Rice N.S.Y. took Patrol of 13 men to OSSUS WOOD, found enemy very alert and somewhat jumpy. A hostile sniper was shot in a tree by 2/Lieut Rice. Two hostile aeroplanes over our line at 6.10.a.m. retired in S.E. direction on being fired on by our A.A. Guns. Heavy firing heard up North at 2.10.p.m. joining trench between H. & C. Communicating Trench started. Wiring at Outpost and deepening on communication trench. Work on trenches in GREEN LINE and wire started between G. & QUARRIES. Casualty :- 3632 Pte GAMBELL R., 3rd Dragoon Guards wounded. Our M.Gs searched back area during the night. OSSUS VILLAGE to S.25.c.5.7. LEMPIRE VILLAGE shelled throughout the day. LITTLE PRIEL FARM shelled intermittently during the day. Four hostile aeroplanes over our lines at 8.25... very high.Went EAST on being shelled. Hostile Patrol advanced on South of QUARRIES., 1 man was seen to be hit and patrol retired. Weather fine.	
	31/3/17		1½ Squadrons 10th Hussars relieved 1½ Squadrons 3rd Dragoon Guards in Support Line. Blues relieved Royals in BROWN LINE. 8th M.G. Squadron relieved 5th M.G. Squadron. 9.45.p.m. till 12. midnight LITTLE PRIEL FARM shelled. EPEHY shelled. LEMPIRE VILLAGE shelled. Royals and 6th M.G. Squadron returned to HUTS. Lieut Clifton Brown, Royals wounded at 1.p.m.	
	1/4/17	9.a.m.	Two Green boxes size of 4 gallon petrol tins. seen from Outpost painted Green with figure H/and some writing. A German examined the boxes and was shot. The boxes could not be obtained owing to the proximity of German trench. Post :- Wiring from C. Post to Outpost continued and French Wire placed from Communication trench to detached post North of QUARRIES. C. communication trench lengthened and improved. Night very quiet. Officers 10th Hussars and Blues came up at 10.p.m. to take over Outpost GREEN LINE and Supports.	
	2/4/17		Weather fine. Quiet day till 5.p.m. when Bosches put in some shells about COPSE 13 and a direct hit in middle of COPSE 12. Retaliation 3 times necessary for Outpost. Our guns shells OSSUS WOOD 6.30.p.m. and eventually caused Bosches to keep very inactive. 1½ Squadrons 10th Hussars relieved 1½ Squadrons 3rd Dragoon Guards in Outpost. Blues relieved N.S.Y. in GREEN LINE. Essex Yeo relieved Blues in BROWN LINE. H.Qrs Blues relieved H.Qrs 3rd D Gds	

(A7099). Wt. W12899/M1293. 750,000. 1/17. D. D. & L., Ltd. Forms/C.2118-14.

Army Form C. 2118.

WAR DIARY
or
INTELLIGENCE SUMMARY.

(Erase heading not required.)

Instructions regarding War Diaries and Intelligence Summaries are contained in F. S. Regs., Part II. and the Staff Manual respectively. Title pages will be prepared in manuscript.

Place	Date	Hour	Summary of Events and Information	Remarks and references to Appendices
	6/4/1?		In COPSE 15, and moved to new Battalion H.Qrs. Work :- Wire from G. to Outpost continued 1 Officer (Lieut Kohler), 250 O.R. left at EPEHY for working party. Lieut Harries and 5 N.C.Os left for 24 hours in Outpost. Casualties :- 15693 Pte ATKINS D., 3rd Dgn Gds. wounded. Relief completed 1.30.a.m. Reported by telephone and personally to G.O.C., 6th Cav Bde. by O.C. D.L.Sector. (sd) Alfred Burt Lieut Colonel, Commanding 3rd Dragoon Guards.	

Army Form C. 2118.

WAR DIARY
or
INTELLIGENCE SUMMARY.
(Erase heading not required.)

3rd Dragoons
Vol 29

Place	Date	Hour	Summary of Events and Information	Remarks and references to Appendices
BUIRE	1919 June 1		HQ and 3 Sqdns still in Line (See appendix to War Diary for May).	WD
"	2		H.Q and the Sqdns were relieved by the 10th Hussars and returned	WD
"	3		back to camp.	WD
"	4		Routine in camp.	WD
"	5		" "	WD
"	6		Captain N. McLachlan proceed to British Cavalry Establishing "Bath" for attachment. Lieut F Bower and two O.Rs ranks commenced French Mortar course at COURCELLES.	WD
"	7		Counter Attack by 1st reserve Bde. & D. Sabre practice.	WD
"	8		Gas course at LONGAVESNES commenced. 1 Lieut. & NKipp and 2.O.R. attend	WD
"	9		Routine in camp.	WD
"	10		" "	WD
"	11		" "	WD

Army Form C. 2118.

WAR DIARY
or
INTELLIGENCE SUMMARY.
(Erase heading not required.)

Instructions regarding War Diaries and Intelligence Summaries are contained in F. S. Regs., Part II. and the Staff Manual respectively. Title pages will be prepared in manuscript.

Place	Date	Hour	Summary of Events and Information	Remarks and references to Appendices
BUIRE	1917 June 10		The Regiment less HQ moves from Camp to D2. Sector. (Appendix)	WD
"	11		Routine in Camp, one man being left to join horses.	WD
"	12		" " "	WD
"	13		" " "	WD
"	14		" " "	WD
"	15		" " "	WD
"	16		" " "	WD
"	17		2/Lieut. T. Kohler proceeds to a Bombing Course. 10 O.R. joins from Rouen.	WD
"	18		Routine in Camp	WD
"	19		" " "	WD
"	20		" " "	WD
"	21		2/Lieut. J. Bowen proceeds to Trench Mortar School at Amiens.	WD
"	22		Routine in Camp.	WD
"	23		" " "	WD
"	24		" " "	WD
"	25		" " "	WD
"	26		" " "	WD

Army Form C. 2118.

WAR DIARY
or
INTELLIGENCE SUMMARY.

(Erase heading not required.)

Instructions regarding War Diaries and Intelligence Summaries are contained in F. S. Regs., Part II. and the Staff Manual respectively. Title pages will be prepared in manuscript.

Place	Date	Hour	Summary of Events and Information	Remarks and references to Appendices
BUIRE.	June 1917. 27		Routine in Camp.	
"	28.		" " "	
"	29		20 Remounts arrived from ROUEN.	
"	30		Routine in Camp.	

M A Quinstan
Capt.
Adjutant. 3rd Dragoon Gds

DIARY FROM 10th JUNE 1917 to JUNE 29th 1917

June 10th. Paraded 6.p.m. Moved off 6.30.p.m. to take over Billets in BROWN LINE (2nd Line). Arrived 8.35.p.m. and met guides. The relief was completed by 9.5.p.m. having taken over from 2nd Life Guards. Wind reported Safe. Men fairly well off for accomodation. Three Gas Guards, of 3 men each. Three Signallers, 6 Runners to Brigade, 2 to Sector Headquarters: Strength of party :- 11 Officers, 322 Other Ranks.

Headquarters	Major G.T.Cliff
	Lieut L.Hellyer
"A" Squadron	Lieut A.B.P.L.Vincent M.C.
	2/Lieut L.F.Bowater
	2/Lieut E.A.L.Kittle
"B" Squadron	Lieut W.G.Bagnell
	Lieut G.R.P.Alsop
	2/Lieut V.Oakley Brown
"C" Squadron	Captain H.P.Holt
	2/Lieut M.V.T.Mott
	2/Lieut R.D.Younger

Very wet night and everybody got wet through.

June 11th. Two Officers, 2/Lieut Steedman and Massey Lynch and 49 Other Ranks rejoined the Regiment from Digging Party at 3.a.m. The morning after 6.a.m. was fine but dull. Wind Safe. About 9.a.m. the day became hot. Nothing happened during the morning, at 1.30.p.m. 2/Lieuts Steedman and Massey Lynch left for Rest Camp.

About 3.p.m. the Guides of the N.S.Y. arrived to take over. At 9.40.p.m. the N.S.Y. came to relieve 3rd Dragoon Guards and the relief was completed by 10.5.p.m., and the Regiment proceeded to relieve the 1st Life Guards in the INTERMEDIATE LINE (GREEN LINE). The relief was completed at 12.15.p.m. without casualties. "A" Squadron in "M" REDOUBT, "B" Squadron in "L" with the Regimental Headquarters "C" Squadron in "K" REDOUBT. All was quiet and the night was fine. Positions see sketch attached. At 1.15.a.m. "C" Squadron from "K" REDOUBT sent out patrol to Outpost Line to get in touch with No 1. Post at X.23.a.5.0., via a connecting post on road at X. 22.d.7.7. This patrol returned about 2.30.a.m. and reported all correct. Work was done on Communication Trenches from 10.30.a.m. to 12.30.p.m.

and 2.30.p.m. to 4.30.p.m., and again at night from 11.p.m. to 3.a.m., when the Stand to took place.

June 12th. The day was fine, an enemy aeroplane came over "L" REDOUBT but went back about 5.a.m. O.C. Sub Sector visited "L" REDOUBT about 4.30.a.m. nothing happened during the morning. Work was proceeded with in trenches. About 2.p.m. a few shells were fired at the Dump on FALLEN TREE ROAD, no hits. About 3.30.p.m. a fire aws seen behind German Lines at the Northern end of HONNECOURT VILLAGE (true bearing from Observation Post 36"). At 5.30.p.m. the Bosches started searching for forward guns just behind "M" REDOUBT after firing about 20 rounds 4 rounds fell into "M" REDOUBT amongst the wire but did no damage. No casualties during the day and the rest of the day passed off quietly. The rations arrived at Dump at 10.30.p.m.

June 13th. Dawn fine. Wind safe. Everything was very quiet. About 7.a.m. 4 high explosives were fired at "L" REDOUBT but fell over by "L" Dump. 7.35.a.m. 5 German aeroplanes came over our line but retired on a barrage of fire being put up. Nothing else happened during the day. Work on Communication trenches continued. At 10.p.m. "C" Squadron from "K" REDOUBT sent out (12 men) covering party for N.S.Y. working party.

June 14th. Nothing doing. Day dawned fine, slight wind which was safe. A few shells dropped near "K" REDOUBT about 10.45.a.m. doing no damage. At 1.55.p.m. our Artillery shelled RANCOURT FARM and the Village of HONNECOURT with good effect. At 3.15.p.m. enemy shelled quarry 3 rounds H.E. 77 mm and at 4.5.p.m. repeated it doing no damage. At 7.30.p.m. a party of enemy 10 strong in half sections at 50 yards interval were observed coming West down road from LE CATELET to PUTNEY. These were followed by a party of 1 platoon in close order. Motor Cars were also observed on the road. The enemy's aeroplanes were active during the evening. During the night the enemy raided working party near No 1 Outpost wounded 3 men of the Royals with bombs and revolvers.

June 15th. Dawn fine but misty. Nothing happened during the morning, everything was quiet. Three men went Sick, the first up here. At 1.p.m. our guns shelled in direction of HONNECOURT WOOD. Target not visible to us on account of misty weather. During the afternoon enemy shelled the road by the FALLEN TREE, direction from whence they came uncertain

Calibre 77.mm and 4.2. The enemy aeroplanes were very quiet
during the day but at 8.30.p.m. a German aeroplane was
observed over D 2 Sub Sector, over "M" POST. Our asroplanes
fairly active. One plane over "M" REDOUBT observing fire, at 8.p
p.m. a large British War plane with 2 propellors circled over
"L" REDOUBT, was shelled by enemy and retired. The Scouts and
Snipers went out at night but with no result. The night was
quiet, a few Star shells were sent up by the enemy.

June 16th.   The day dawned misty but fine. Wind safe, but
by 6.a.m. it changed to Dangerous. About 8.45.a.m. 4 British
and 1 hostile planes over. At 9.a.m. enemy fired 5 shells
into "M" REDOUBT, 4 were duds but destroyed about 5 yards of
trench, at 1.45.p.m. they shelled "L" POST, 2 roads
77.mm, no damage. At 5.45.p.m. 2 observers were seen to
descend from enemy's observation balloon by parashutes, just
East of RANCOURT FARM. At 8.10.p.m. another hostile observation
balloon appeared (true bearing 63" taken from X.21.b.3.8.).
The working parties continued the same as usual on Communication trenches between "L" & "M" POSTS and "L" & "K" POSTS and
the trench to No 1 Outpost. The whole of the day was very
quiet and the night went off without any incident of note.

June 17th.   The dawn was fine.Wind dangerous.The morning was
quiet.About 9.55.a.m.,enemy shelled in the vicinity of "L" Post,
77.mm,H.E.,blowing in a traverse close to the Bomb Store in
"M" Redoubt,about 12.10,a shell landed in "L" Redoubt and blew
in a portion,no casualties.The shelling seemed to come from the
direction of CANAL WOOD.True bearing 67".Again shelled at 2.20
p.m.,and 5.15 p.m.,but no damage done.Too many spectators
walking about on top.Our Aeroplanes were active during the day
a patrol of 8 met 7 German planes about 1000 yards E.of K.,
Redoubt,fighting ensued in which a German aeroplane was hit and
came down in flames (apparently by German anti-aircraft).The
plane fell just inside the German Lines about 1500 yards N.E.
of CATELET COPSE.The Pilot was seen to fall out of the machine
and was carried away in a stretcher.The enemy sent up two fresh
observation Ballons,true bearings 17" & 62" from "L" Post Hd:
Qrts:.All bearings mentioned taken from X.22.c6.4.The rest of
the night was normal.The relief commenced at 11.5.p.m.,and
completed at 1.30.a.m.,"M" Post being first releived then "L"
& "K" .The Regiment was releived from intermediate line by the
ROYALS.On releif the Regiment marched back to the 2nd line at

4.

PEZIERES, reaching that place at 3.15 a.m. No casualties occurred during the relief or during our tour of Duty in the GREEN LINE.

JUNE 18th. Very fine day, nothing doing. One enemy aeroplane came over us and one shell was fired into EPEHY. At 9.15.p.m. the following working parties paraded, Lieut: M.V.T.Mott and 2/Lieut: L.F.Bowater and 100 men on wiring from "K" Post to No 1.Outpost. 2/Lieut: V.Oakley Brown & 75 men on digging communication trench from "L" Redoubt to Pigeon Ravine, they returned about 2.30.a.m. One casualty caused by a pick going in a man's hand (Pte: Ashby. "B" Squadron).

JUNE 19th. The day dawned wet, wind safe. The whole of the day passed off quietly. Only one shell into EPEHY at 11.30.a.m. Working parties told off as follows:- Lieut: G.R.P.Alsop, 2/Lt: L.F.Bowater and 100 men. 2/Lieut: E.A.L.Kittle and 40 men. At 7.p.m. orders came down that "C" Squadron had to take over "K" Redoubt to relieve ROYALS for the Raid. This Squadron paraded at 10.15.p.m., and the relief was completed without any casualties. At 12.M.N.Capt: H.P.Holt, Lieut: M.V.T.Mott, & 2/Lieut R.D.Younger with 76 men went with "C" Squadron in consequence of "C" Squadron having to go into the intermediate line, the working parties were reduced, every man being taken, servants were put on Gas Guard, another party was told off to the Tunnelling Coy: in Pigeon Ravine, leaving only 127 Officers, N.C.O's,& men in 2nd line (Brown Line). The working parties returned about 2.a.m., without casualties.

JUNE 20th. Fine to start with, but thunder-storms during the day. Wind safe. 2 Hotchkiss Rifles told off to practice the Raid with the ROYALS,1 from "A" Squadron & 1.from "B" Squadron. After the enemy had shelled the Village of EPEHY at 9.55.a.m., with four rounds, the rest of the day was quiet. 2/Lieut: W.H. Stork joined for duty. Working parties as follows:- 2/Lieut: W.H.Stork & 40 men from 3.p.m. to 6.30.p.m. 2/Lieut: V.Oakley Brown & 2/Lieut: E.A.L.Kittle & 60 men from 10.15.p.m. to 2.30.p.m., they returned without casualties.

JUNE 21st. Dawn fine, but dull. Wind safe. Intermittent shelling of EPEHY from 6.30.a.m. to 9.30.a.m. from the direction N.E., no damage was done. Rest of the day quiet. Heavy rain during the afternoon. Working parties from 9.15.p.m. to 2.30.a.m. Lieut: G. R.P.Alsop & 2/Lieut: W.H.Stork with 100 men digging communication trench from "L" Redoubt tp Pigeon Ravine. They returned at at 2.30.a.m. without any casualties.

June 22nd. Fine, Wind safe. The day passed without incident Rain most of the day. At night the usual working party went out at 9.15.p.m. till 2.a.m., 2/Lieut L.F.Bowater, 2/Lieut V.Oakley Brown, and 100. Other Ranks. There were no casualties.

June 23rd. The dawn was fine, wind safe. The Colonel came to visit the Regiment in the morning. Everything was quiet during the day. At 9.30.p.m. the Regiment paraded to relieve the N.S.Y. in the Outpost Line. "A" Squadron and 2 troops "B" Squadron (No1 & No 2) went into the Outpost Line. "A" Squadron, Lieut A.B.P.L.Vincent M.C., 2/Lieut L.F.Bowater, 2/Lieut E.A.L.Kittle, 2/Lieut W.H. Stork and 90 men into the Outpost Line. Lieut G.R.P.Alsop and the 2 troops of "B" Squadron (40 men) into local support, 1 troop on SUNKEN ROAD, near new Outpost H.Qrs, 1 troop in QUARRY. Headquarters consisting of Major G.T. Cliff, Lieut L.Hellyer, and 19 men into the QUARRIES. "C" Squadron and 2 troops of "B" Squadron moved into the new Outpost support line, which was the Communication Trench between "K" & "L" POST and the Short Trench behind "M" POST ("B" Squadron). "C" Squadron, Captain H.P.Holt, Lieut M.V.T. Mott, and 2/Lieut R.D.Younger. "B" Squadron Lieut W.G.Bagnell, and 2/Lieut V.Oakley Brown. The relief was completed by 1.20.a.m. without casualties, all was very quiet. Work was at once commenced on positions and fire trenches which were in a very bad state (undercut) drainage and a trench was dug across SUNKEN ROAD, running between 3 POST and 2 POST (X.2.3.b.1.7.).

June 24th. Beautiful dawn. wind safe. Enemy's aeroplanes active all day especially bewteen 3.30.p.m. and 4.30.p.m. when two planes flew very low over Outpost Line and were dri driven off by M.G. fire. In the evening a hostile aircraft came over and was heavily shelled by our anti aircraft. It went away towards CANAL WOOD very shakily, probably hit. The enemy shelled "L" REDOUBT slightly during the day The line as a whole was quiet during the day. At 1.a.m. the Royals did a raid starting from 2 points at No 1 POST and No 2 POST to them were attached 3 Hotchkiss Rifles from 3rd Dragoon Guards, 2 from "B" and 1 from "A", from "B" Squadron, Corporals Stokes and Tyler, willis and

Ball, from "A" Corporal Coles and Casburn, and also the Regimental snipers. The Regiment was ordered to have the wire cut and marking tapes out by 1.a.m. This was done by Lieut A.B.P.L.Vincent M.C. and at 12.45.p.m. Lieut L.Hellyer reported that all was ready and guides provided. At 1.10.a.m. the raid started. Our Machine Guns shooting in direct fire on CANAL WOOD and OSSUS WOOD and our Artillery putting up a barrage (lifting) in front of raiding party. The raid was conducted by Lieut Colonel Wormald D.S.O. Royals, and went in 2 parties. The right hand party entered the new trench and killed 1. The left party was held up by the Bosches wire. At 1.28.a.m. a signal (Green Rocket) recalled the raiders. The Huns put up, first a barrage of Trench Mortars and Rifle Grenades and then used Shrapnell. The raid was over by 2.a.m. and all was quiet by 2.15.a.m. The casualties were rather heavy 3rd Dragoon Guards losing Sergt Hicks and L/Corporal Boast killed, of the wounded no report has yet been received. They are being buried at VILLERS FAUCON this afternoon. Although the Bosches put up a big barrage, only 1 shell landed in our Outpost Line doing no damage. Work done during the day, deepening, draining, parapets made in trenches, wall and shelters built in QUARRIES.

June 25th.   Dawn fine wind safe. All quiet. We rather expected some strafeing after the raid but were disappointed. About 7.20 a.m. enemy fired at the QUARRY no damage, and also fired 3 rounds at "M" POST from the direction of CANAL WOOD. There was aerial activity on both sides, 1 enemy plane coming very low over the QUARRY. Evidently an explosion occurred at VENDHUILE for a large column of smoke was seen going up for an hour (bearing) 121 " taken from QUARRY. The rest of the day and night was quiet. Work done, improvements in bivouacs, in QUARRIES, repairing and deepening of trenches in No 3 POST. Party of 100 men from Intermediate support wiring in front of Nos 3 & 4 POSTS. Enemy got the wind up at 1.a.m., 26th, and VERY LIGHTS were numerous. Red Lights followed by Green Rockets were repeatedly sent up. M.G. fire from OSSUS and CANAL WOODS, and No 3 POST shelled but no harm done, numerous fires were seen in OSSUS VILLAGE. 2/Lieut J.Massey-Lynch joined for duty.

June 26th.   Dawn fine wind safe, All the morning was quiet

except for a little shelling by the Bosches at about 8.45.
a.m. to 10.a.m. when he shelled from No 1 to the QUARRIES
twice and 9.45.a.m. "K" & "L" POSTS were also shelled
direction of fire from CANAL WOOD. When our batteries
commenced shelling ceased. The enemy aeroplanes were very
active especially over No 3 POST and the QUARRY, flying
very low. At about 7.40.p.m. 5 Bosches planes reconnoitred t
the Outpost Line, a Squadron of ours came out later and
the Huns cleared off about 8.10.p.m. There were 21 planes
in view for a quarter of an hour. About 8.30.p.m. the huns
started registering on No 3 POST wire and continued up to
9.30.p.m., and about 9.46.p.m. an enemy plane flew over.
This made me think (combined with the aeroplanes in the
morning) a raid might be coming on No 3 POST, but none
came. All the rest of the night was quiet, except for short
bursts of M.G. fire. Work done, improving trenches in
X.22.c.. At 10.30.p.m. the relief of "A" Squadron and half "B/
Squadron. The relief was completed at 12.15.p.m. without
any casualties, "C" Squadron, Captain H.P.Holt, Lieut M.V.T
Mott, 2/Lieut R.D.Younger and 99. Other Ranks. The rest of
the night was quiet. Two men of "C" Squadron went sick
during the day, Ptes Coxhead and Seymour. 2/Lieut J.P.Brill
joined for duty.

June 27th. Dawn wet wind safe. About noon our batteries
shelled OSSUS WOOD and againa t 12.30.p.m.. Before this
however the enemy had shelled Outpost Line and the Quarry,
direction of fire from BANTOUZZLE. About midday the enemy
passed over BIRDCAGE but was driven off by anti aircraft.
It rained hard during the afternoon and the evening. About
9.p.m. Outpost shelled also PIGEON RAVINE. Our batteries
replied and shelled OSSUS later on ground X.17.d.6.4.
Work done, improving Outpost Line. Rest of the night was
very quiet, bur very wet. An Officer of the 4th Hussars
came to look round preparatory to taking over on the 28th/
29th.

June 28th The dawn was wet and the wind turning to
dangerous. The enemy shelled the Outpost Line from 7.a.m.,
at 10.30.a.m. PIGEON RAVINE also shelled, direction of fire
from LA TERRIERE. The rest of the day was quiet, just an odd
shell was fired. At 5.20.p.m. 2 enemy planes came over the

QUARRY, directly afterwards, the enemy started shelling the QUARRY and No 2 Outpost. Two shells alanded right in the QUARRY wounding 4 men, Sergt Marsh, Ptes Cox, Stephenson, Tarrant. A little later 1 landed in No 3 POST wounding 2/Lieut J.P.Brill. All the wounded were evacuated at dusk. It rained hard all the evening. Guides were sent to the barrier at 1o.15.p.m. to meet the 4th Hussars who were to relieve us. At 11.10.p.m. the relief commenced and was completed without casualty. At 12.20.a.m. the Regiment marched back to EPEHY where the horses were waiting and arrived in Camp at BUIRE about 5.30.a.m. June 29th.

June 29/6/17   (sd) G.T.Cliff   Major
                         Commanding 3rd Dragoon Guards Detachment.

WAR DIARY or INTELLIGENCE SUMMARY.

Army Form C. 2118.

Vol 30 3o Dragoon Guards

Place	Date	Hour	Summary of Events and Information	Remarks and references to Appendices
BUIRE	1.7.17		Routine in Camp.	WD/b
BUIRE	2.7.17		March Orders received to move to new billeting area	WD/b
	3.7.17		Regiment with Echelons A & B marched to SUZANNE	WD/b
	4.7.17		Regiment with Echelon A marched at 8AM to BUIRE-SUS-CORBIE Echelon B marched at 9AM for same destination	WD/b
	5.7.17		Regiment with Echelon A & B marched from BUIRE-SOUS-CORBIE 7:30am for ORVILLE	WD/b
	6.7.17		Regiment remained at ORVILLE	WD/b
	7.7.17		Regiment with A & B Echelon marched from ORVILLE at 10.30AM for ETREE.	WD/b
	8.7.17		Regiment remained the day at ETREE.	WD/b
	9.7.17		Regiment with B & A Echelons paraded at 8.30 AM for the forward march to MARLES-LES-MINES	WD/b
	10.7.17		Regiment arranced at MARLES-LES MINES. The D.G.O. inspected S.B. respirators of Regiment.	WD/b
MARLES-Les MINES	11.7.17		Routine in Billets	WD/b
"	12.7.17		Routine in Camp	WD/b
"	13.7.17		Routine in Billets. The G.O.C. inspected Recruits & Remounts of Regiment	WD/b
"	14.7.17		Routine in Billets	WD/b

Army Form C. 2118.

WAR DIARY
or
INTELLIGENCE SUMMARY.

(Erase heading not required.)

30 Seaforth Trunks

Place	Date	Hour	Summary of Events and Information	Remarks and references to Appendices
MARLES les MINES	15.7.17		Routine in Billets. Divisional Service was held at 9.30AM	W.T.b
	16.7.17		The Regiment proceeded at 4.AM for the forward move to LE CORBIE	W.T.b
LE CORBIE	17.7.17		Settling down in new area	W.T.b
"	18.7.17		Routine in Billets	W.T.b
"	19.7.17		Routine in Billets. G.O.C inspected A Echelon of the Regiment	W.T.b
"	20.7.17		Routine in Billets G.O.C. inspected fighting troops cyclists in Marching Order.	W.T.b
"	21.7.17		Routine in Billets	
"	22.7.17		Routine in Billets Divine Service was held at 9.15AM	W.T.b
"	23.7.17		The Regiment proceeded to Rifle Range at ROMBLY for musketry	W.T.b
"	24.7.17		Routine in Billets. Capt MORE. 1 Officer + 1 N.C.O per squadron unit 2 Hotchkiss teams per squadron proceeded to CAMIERS for course lasting till 29.7.17.	W.T.b
"	25.7.17		Routine in Billets 13 Remounts received	W.T.b
"	26.7.17		Routine in Billets. 2/Lt W.H. STARK and 1.NCO per squadron to Physical Training School St.POL for course	W.T.b
"	27.7.17		Routine in Billets	W.T.b

Army Form C. 2118.

WAR DIARY
or
INTELLIGENCE SUMMARY.
(Erase heading not required.)

Place	Date	Hour	Summary of Events and Information	Remarks and references to Appendices
LE CORBIE	28.7.17		Routine in Billets	
"	29.7.17		Routine in Billets. Divine Service was held at 10.15 AM	
"	30.7.17		Routine in Billets	
"	31.7.17		Routine in Billets. Brigade Aquatic Sports.	

WAR DIARY
INTELLIGENCE SUMMARY.

(Erase heading not required.)

Army Form C. 2118.

3rd Dragoon Guards
Vol 31

Place	Date	Hour	Summary of Events and Information	Remarks and references to Appendices
L.E. CORBIE.	1-8-17		Routine in billets.	WAR
	2-8-17		"	WAR
	3		"	WAR
	4		"	WAR
	5		"	WAR
	6		Major H.A. Rycroft and 11 O.R. attended a Commemoration Service in the Château grounds at RANCHICOURT.	WAR
	7		A Divisional Rifle Meeting was held at RANBLY. Capt. N. Neal, More and 50 O.R. proceeded to Army fr work.	WAR
	8		Sniping Course at BILVIC opened.	WAR
	9		Routine in Billets	WAR
	10		"	WAR
	11		Inspection by A.D.M.S. A hostile air-raid was carried out in the evening.	WAR
	12		Routine in Billets.	WAR
	13		"	WAR
	14		"	WAR
	15		Another Air raid took place	WAR
	16		... on FIRE RANGE.	WAR

Army Form C. 2118.

3rd Dragoon Guards

WAR DIARY
or
INTELLIGENCE SUMMARY.
(Erase heading not required.)

Instructions regarding War Diaries and Intelligence Summaries are contained in F. S. Regs., Part II. and the Staff Manual respectively. Title pages will be prepared in manuscript.

Place	Date	Hour	Summary of Events and Information	Remarks and references to Appendices
LE CORBIE	1st		Routine in Billets	WA1
"	21		Pipe Signalling Scheme	WA5
"	22		Inspection of Transport by O.C. A.S.C.	WA5
"	23		Eliminating trials held by Regt. for Bde. Horse Show	WA5
"	24		Eliminating trials held by Bde. for Div. Horse Show	WA5
"	25		Eliminating trials held by Division for Corps Horse Show (team finals – 3 seconds)	WA1
"	26		Routine in Billets. Capt. Mu and 50 O.R. returns from Army (solo finals – 2 seconds)	WA5
"	27		Gas Course at AIRE commences	WA5
"	28			
"	29			
"	30		Routine in Billets	
"	31			

H.A. Grimshaw
Capt.
Adjutant, 3rd Dragoon Guards

Army Form C. 2118.

WAR DIARY
or
INTELLIGENCE SUMMARY.
(Erase heading not required.)

September 1917
3rd Bn. Suffolk

Vol 32

Place	Date	Hour	Summary of Events and Information	Remarks and references to Appendices
LE CORBIE	Sept. 1.		Routine in Billets.	A/14
"	2.			
"	3.		Lieut. J. Kohler and 1 NCO per Sqdn commenced a bombing course at XI Corps.	A/15 A/14
"	4.		Seven Remounts arrived.	A/01
"	5.		Routine in Billets.	A/15
"	6.		—	A/17
"	7.		—	A/17
"	8.		—	A/17
"	9.		Regt Run. Our Competition.	A/17
"	10.		Routine in Billets.	A/05
"	11.		—	A/05
"	12.		Pte Larned Escorted.	A/05
"	13.		Captain J.T. Gibbs joined from England.	A/05
"	14.		Routine in Billets.	A/07
"	15.		Regt Rifle Meeting at LINGHEM.	A/17
"	16.		Routine in Billets	A/17

Army Form C. 2118.

WAR DIARY
or
INTELLIGENCE SUMMARY.
(Erase heading not required.)

3rd Dragoon Guards
September 1917
Sheet 2

Place	Date	Hour	Summary of Events and Information	Remarks and references to Appendices
LE CROISIE	Sept 17		2/Lieut Q.W. Whitton and 3 N.C.O.s Commence Trench Mortar Course.	WAG
"	18		Regtl Tactical Exercise.	WAG
"	19		Sen. O.R. Transfers to Infantry.	WAG
"	20		Routine in Billets.	WAG
"	21		Bde. Tactical Exercise.	WAG
"	22		Divisional Jumping Competition. 2/Lieut. R.D. Younger joins in class.	WAG
"	23		Routine in Billets.	WAG
"	24		" " "	WAG
"	25		" " "	WAG
"	26		" " "	WAG
"	27		" " "	WAG
"	28		" " "	WAG
"	29		Sgt Barker proceeds to Hotchkiss Rifle School at Touquet. Sgt Alexander to 1st Army Sniping School.	WAG
"	30			WAG

W.A. Grimshaw
Col
O/in/Comd 3rd Dragoon Guards

WAR DIARY or INTELLIGENCE SUMMARY

Army Form C. 2118.

October 1917

3rd Dragoon Guards

Place	Date	Hour	Summary of Events and Information	Remarks and references to Appendices
LE SART.	Oct 1st		Lieut B.H. Osmaston and 1 NCO to Sniping School at Linghem. Lieut L.F. Bowater and 3 NCO's to Trench Mortar Course, Neuville. 17 O.R. Transfers to the Infantry. 10 to Bean Review. Routine in Billets.	WM1 WM1 WM8 WM8
"	2nd		"	WM5
"	3rd		Bde Tactical Exercise. Routine in Billets.	WM8
"	4th		Divine Service 11.15 am at LE SART. Regt Signal Troop formed and attached to H.Qrs. Routine in Billets.	WM8 WM6
"	5th			WM6
"	6th			WM2
"	7th		Major H.A. Ryceroft to 6th Cav. Bde. Routine in Billets.	WM8
"	8th		"	WM7
"	9th		"	WM6
"	10th		"	WM2
"	11th			WM4
"	12th		Divine Service at LE SART. 2/Lieut W.C. McErwin and 3 NCO's to Trench Mortar Course at NEUVILLE. Routine in Billets.	
"	13th			
"	14th			
"	15th			WM4
"	16th			WM4
"	17th			WM4
"	18th			
"	19th			
"	20th		The Regt marched from HAVERSKERQUE, LE SART, area and moved to HESTRUS.	
HESTRUS	21st		The Regt remains at HESTRUS.	WM9

Sheet II

October 1917

Army Form C. 2118.

3rd Dragoon Guards

WAR DIARY
INTELLIGENCE SUMMARY.
(Erase heading not required.)

Instructions regarding War Diaries and Intelligence Summaries are contained in F. S. Regs., Part II. and the Staff Manual respectively. Title pages will be prepared in manuscript.

Place	Date	Hour	Summary of Events and Information	Remarks and references to Appendices
HESTRUS	Oct 22		The Regt. marched to Vacquerie-Le-Bourcq where it billeted for night.	WD
VACQUERIE LE BOURCQ	23.		The Regt moved to RIBEAUCOURT, FRANSU, FRANKVILLE AREA and remained for night.	WD
RIBEAUCOURT	24th		The Regt continued the march to LONGPRÉ, and arrived about 12:30pm	WD
LONGPRÉ	25th		Improvement of Billets	WD
"	26th			WD
"	27th		A dismounted party of 4 Offs and 97 OR to DOINGT. To buy stores.	WD
"	28th		Routine in Billets. "B" Sqdn moved to L'ÉTOILE	WD
"	29th		Class of Instruction for Young Officers commenced.	WD
"	30th		Routine in Billets.	WD
"	31st			WD

W A Grimshaw
Captain
Adjutant, 3rd Dragoon Guards.

WAR DIARY or INTELLIGENCE SUMMARY

3rd D.R. from front Army Form C. 2118.
1 to 22nd NOVEMBER 1917

Vol 34

Place	Date	Hour	Summary of Events and Information	Remarks and references to Appendices
LONGPRÉ	Nov 1		Routine in Billets.	WD9
"	2		" " "	WD9
"	3		" " "	WD9
"	4		" " "	WD9
"	5		Divine Service 11:30 am.	WD9
"	6		" " "	WD9
"	7		" " "	WD9
"	8		Lieut G.E. Lewison and 3 O.R's to P.S.B.T. School	WD9
"	9		Routine in Billets.	WD9
"	10		" " "	WD9
"	11		" " "	WD9
"	12		" " "	WD9
"	13		1. O.R. to 3rd Army Musketry School.	WD9
"	14		2. Officers & S.O.R. drawn (by 6 NZ Sqdn) has to adapt & fix a Jemmam M.Q.	WD9
"	15		Routine in Billets.	WD9
"	16		" " "	WD9
FRANVILLERS	17		The Regiment marches to FRANVILLERS where it reviewed the night	WD9
"	18		" " "	WD9
CAPPY	19		The Regiment moved at 4:30 pm to CAPPY and went into Billets.	WD9
"	20		Regiment Stood to at 1/2 hour before to night.	WD9
"	21		Regiment Stood to at 1 hour " "	WD9
"	22		" " " " " "	WD9

WAR DIARY
or
INTELLIGENCE SUMMARY.

Army Form C. 2118.

3rd Dragoon Guards

November 1917

Place	Date	Hour	Summary of Events and Information	Remarks and references to Appendices
HÉRISSART.	Nov 23		The Regiment moves to HÉRISSART & PUCHEVILLERS	
"	24		Routine in Billets.	
"	25		"	
"	26		"	
"	27		"	
"	28		"	
"	29		"	
"	30		Advance Party to TINCOURT moves up by Bus but recalled down night 30/11/17	

7-12-17

N.A. Grimshaw
Captain.
Adjutant. 3rd Dragoon Guards.

WAR DIARY
or
INTELLIGENCE SUMMARY.
(Erase heading not required.)

Army Form C. 2118.

3rd Dragoon Guards
Vol 35

Place	Date	Hour	Summary of Events and Information	Remarks and references to Appendices
HERISSART	Dec 1917 1.		A Mounted Party consisting of 8 Officers and 218 OR entrained at HERISSART at 6.30 am and proceed to HANGOURT where it remained le. War	WAQ
"	2.		A Working Party of 250 OR under Captain W.G. Baguli proceed to HANGOURT	WAQ
"	3.		The Party continued work under Capt. J.T. Gibbs.	WAQ
"	4.		"	WAQ
"	5.		The Dism'd Batln. Stood To in Camp.	WAQ
"	6.		Covered Party took over Sector of front line Trenches	WAQ
"	7.		HQ Sqn marched from HANGOURT to VADENGOURT, and took over line from	WAQ
"	8.		Rifle Bde.	WAQ
"	9.		Line Quiet. Patrols under dr Katinako.	WAQ
"	10.		Patrols sent out.	WAQ
"	11.		Situation Quiet. Cpl Lindsay killed. Capt Baguli and Pte Robb wounded.	WAQ
"	12.		A Patrol of the 3rd Dragoon Guards captured a German automatic rifle	WAQ
"	13.		Situation Quiet.	WAQ
"	14.		"	WAQ
"	15		Enemy aircraft busy.	WAQ

Army Form C. 2118.

3d Dragoon Guards

WAR DIARY
INTELLIGENCE SUMMARY.
(Erase heading not required.)

Instructions regarding War Diaries and Intelligence Summaries are contained in F. S. Regs., Part II. and the Staff Manual respectively. Title pages will be prepared in manuscript.

Place	Date	Hour	Summary of Events and Information	Remarks and references to Appendices
HERISSART	Dec 1916 16		Situation quiet.	
"	17		Heavy Snow fell, patrols were not sent out	
"	18		Situation quiet.	
"	19		Lt Thomson R de R. relieved by 7th (Res) Bde & sent into reserve.	
"	20		Capt Gibbs relieved by Capt W.P. Stern in charge of C.S.M.	
"	21		Horses moved from HERISSART to AILLY-LE-HAUT-CLOCHER.	
AILLY	22		Remainder in billets.	
"	23			
"	24		Officers & men refugees from Batn HQrs.	
"	25		S.O.R. to Batt HQrs.	
"	26		Remainder in billets.	
"	27			
"	28			
"	29			
"	30			
"	31			

H.A.Gimsham
Captain
Adjutant 3d Dragoon Gds.

WAR DIARY
INTELLIGENCE SUMMARY.
(Erase heading not required.)

Army Form C. 2118.

Instructions regarding War Diaries and Intelligence Summaries are contained in F. S. Regs., Part II. and the Staff Manual respectively. Title pages will be prepared in manuscript.

Place	Date	Hour	Summary of Events and Information	Remarks and references to Appendices
AILLY-LE-HAUT-CLO-CHER.	1918 Nov 1		Routine in Billets	APX
	2		Lieut E.G. Stedman releives N.T. King 1/2 Divis. M.G. Opt. anp. Procuded to Div. School	APX
	3		Routine in Billets	APX
	4		" " "	APX
	5		" " "	APX
	6		" " "	APX
	7		" " "	APX
	8		Regt. Headquarters releives Maj. M Somerset Yeomanry in the Trenches. Lt R.G.S. Shepley releives proceeded to Cav Corps Sqdn for signal course	APX
	9		Routine in Billets	APX
	10		Relieved Personnel from Battn Sqdn disemb'd Rys returned to Billets	APX
	11		Routine in Billets	APX
	12		" " "	APX
	13		" " "	APX
	14		" " "	APX
	15		S.S.M. Halliday and 4 O.R. Killed in Railway Accident, returns to France	APX
	16		Regt. H.Qrs and Disms Pers returned to Billets	APX
	17		Routine in Billets	APX
	18		" " "	APX
	19		" " "	APX

Army Form C. 2118.

WAR DIARY
or
INTELLIGENCE SUMMARY.
(Erase heading not required.)

3. Dragoon Guards

WA 36

Place	Date	Hour	Summary of Events and Information	Remarks and references to Appendices
AILLY-LE-HAUT CLOCHER	Jan 21		Routine in Billets.	WAG
"	22		" " "	WAG
"	23		" " "	WAG
"	24		" " "	WAG
"	25		Pioneer Sqdn proceeded to huts in relief Domn. Sqdn	WAG
"	26		Remain in Billets.	WAG
"	27		" " "	WAG
"	28		The Regiment marched to LA CHAUSSÉ and went into billets.	WAG
LA CHAUSSE	29			WAG
MARCELCAVE	30		The Regiment moved to MARCELCAVE.	WAG
TERTRY	31		The Regiment continuing the march to TERTRY, the final area. Building up of Stores.	WAG

WA Quinton
Captain
Adjutant 3rd Dragoon Guards

Army Form C. 2118.

WAR DIARY
INTELLIGENCE SUMMARY.
(Erase heading not required.)

3. Brafordial

Place	Date	Hour	Summary of Events and Information	Remarks and references to Appendices
TERTRY	Feb 1918 13.		Routine in Billets.	MAA 8
"	14.		"	MAA 8
"	15.		"	MAA 8
"	16.		3 Officers and 116 O.R. proceeded to Jeancourt to work on Green Line.	MAA 8
"	17.		"	MAA 8
"	18.		"	MAA 9
"	19.		"	MAA 9
"	20.		Course. 2/Lieut. F.S. BRETELL to T.M. School.	MAA 9
"	21.		"	MAA 9
"	22.		"	MAA 9
"	23.		" Lieut. P.Q.Q. Warren to Pigeon Course.	MAA 9
"	24.		"	MAA 9
"	25.		"	MAA 9
"	26.		"	MAA 9
"	27.		"	MAA 9
"	28.		"	MAA 9

During the whole of this period the Regt. was required to find about 100 diggers daily.

H.H.Quinlan Capt
Adjutant 3 Dragoon Gds.

WAR DIARY
INTELLIGENCE SUMMARY

Army Form C. 2118.

3rd Dragoon Guards

Vol 37

Place	Date	Hour	Summary of Events and Information	Remarks and references to Appendices
TERTRY.	1918 FEB. 1		Routine in Billets.	
"	2		"	
"	3		"	
"	4		"	
"	5		"	
"	6		Honours — 19889 Sqt Johnson G. 19927 A/Cpl SEALE. 12944 A/Cpl McDONALD } Croix de Guerre (Belgian)	WAR Q. WAR Q. WAR Q.
"	7		Courses — Lieut. R.D. Younger, Lieut. T. Kohler, Lieut. N.J. Macey-Lynch } To 3rd Cav Div School.	WAR Q. WAR Q.
"	8		" Lieut. W.G. Opthorpe, Lieut. G.M. Whitton } To Pigeon Course.	WAR Q.
"	9		Courses — Major G.T. Cliff, V Army S.O.S. School.	WAR Q.
"	10		Lieut. P.G.A. Weaver, Killed in riding accident.	WAR Q.
"	11		Reinforcements — Capt. O.K. Benton, 2/Lieut. F.S. Brettell } Joined Regt.	WAR Q. WAR Q.
"	12		2/Lieut. R.G. Roden, Joined Regt.	WAR Q.

6th Bat 6/3
3 Dn 3 Dragoon Guards Vol 38

WAR DIARY
INTELLIGENCE SUMMARY

Army Form C. 2118.

Place	Date	Hour	Summary of Events and Information	Remarks and references to Appendices
TERTRY.	March 1918		March. Routine in Billets	
	2			WD
	3			WD
	4			WD
	5			
	6			
	7		The Regt. stood to from March 7th – 10.9am Rr. of 9th	WD
	8			WD
	9		The Regt was no longer required & stood to. Re being done by Each Yeomany.	WD
	10		Routine in Billets	WD
	11			WD
	12			WD
	13		The Regt moved from TERTRY to DEVISE	WD
DEVISE.	14		Routine in Billets 18 O.R. joined from Rouen	WD
	15			WD
	16			WD
	17			WD
	18			WD

WAR DIARY

INTELLIGENCE SUMMARY

Army Form C. 2118.

3rd Dragoons

Place	Date	Hour	Summary of Events and Information	Remarks and references to Appendices
DEVISE	March 19		Rounds in Billets	WAR
"	20		"	WAR
"	21		The Regt marched from DEVISE to BEAUMONT, and on arrival formed part of the 6th Dismtd Bde under Colonel Burne. Was 3rd Dragoon Gds. 3L Regt. entrained & took over the line near NOUROUIL-VIRY under 173 Inf. Bde.	WAR
BEAUMONT	22		The Regt dug in in support of front line ie E of NOUREUIL VIRY	None
"	23		Enemy attacked village from the North and succeeded in getting a footing in village	WAR
"	24-28th		Active Operations, Coup. of which attacked. There were near to TRACY LE MONT & disms Bde which rejoining reinforced ? Bde the same day.	WAR Appendix
"	28"			
CHOISY AU BAC	29"		Stood to at 5·45 am.	WAR
"	30.		Stood to at 5·45 am and moved off to AIRON, a distance of about 23 miles, arriving about 11 am.	WAR
"	31		Left AIRON at 5·30 am and proceeded to BURY about 8 miles away.	WAR

Adjutant MacGinnchen Capt
3rd Dragoon Gds

6th Cav.Bde.
3rd Cav.Div.

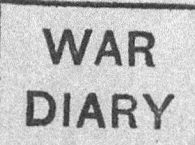

3rd DRAGOON GUARDS.

A P R I L

1 9 1 8

INTELLIGENCE SUMMARY.

(Erase heading not required.)

3rd Dragoon Guards
WR 39

Place	Date	Hour	Summary of Events and Information	Remarks and references to Appendices
SAINS-EN-AMIENOIS In the field	April 1918 1.		The whole division was billeted in our large farm. Stood to at 5.45am.	WAR
	2.		Stood to at 5.45am and moved to BOIS DE GENTELLES, and later to a wood (N.34.c.62D), where the Regiment bivouacked.	WAR
	3.		Stood to at 5.45am and moved off to Bois. L'ABBAYE.	WAR
	4.		Stood to at 5.45am and ordered up to support XIV Division which was coming back. The situation was very obscure and a new line dug which was handed over to the Australians the next day. Position maintained, two attacks beaten off etc. The Regiment was relieved by Australians.	WAR
	5.		The Regiment attempted in wood in N.34.c	WAR
CAMON	6.		CAMON. 12 Officers, 76 O.R. & 56 horses belonging to Regt as reinforcements.	WAR
	7.		14 Reinforcements received. Routine in billets.	WAR
	8.			WAR
	9.		Memorial Service held for men killed in recent fighting.	WAR

INTELLIGENCE SUMMARY.

(Erase heading not required)

3. Dragoon Gds

Place	Date	Hour	Summary of Events and Information	Remarks and references to Appendices
CAMON	April 1918 10.		Routine in Billets	WAy
"	11		The Regiment less B Echelon march to ROUGEFAY where it billets the night.	WAy
ROUGEFAY	12		The Regiment continued its march to EPPS when it billets the night	WAy
EPPS.	13		It march continued to BAILLEUL LES PERNES.	WAy
BAILLEUL LES PERNES.	14		Routine in Billets.	WAy
"	15		"	WAy
"	16		"	WAy
"	17		Lieut-Colonel C.L ROME. 11th Hussars assumed command of Regt vice Lieut Colonel A. Burr DSO to 7th Cavalry Bde	WAy
"	18		Routine in Billets.	WAy
"	19		"	WAy
"	20.		8.O.R. D train received	WAy
"	21.		"	WAy
"	22		"	WAy
"	23		"	WAy
"	24		"	WAy
"	25		Division Conference.	WAy

INTELLIGENCE SUMMARY.

(Erase heading not required.)

Place	Date	Hour	Summary of Events and Information	Remarks and references to Appendices
BAILLEUL LES PERNES.	April 26		Routine in Billets. Bde Signalling Scheme	WAS
"	27		" " "	WAS
"	28		" " "	WAS
"	29		" " "	WAS
"	30		2 Officers and 10 OR horses joined from Autheville	WAS

M.A. Grimshaw
Capt.
Adjutant 3rd Dragoon Guards

Army Form C. 2118.

3rd Dragoon Guards
May 1918

WG 170

WAR DIARY
or
INTELLIGENCE SUMMARY.
(Erase heading not required.)

Instructions regarding War Diaries and Intelligence Summaries are contained in F. S. Regs., Part II. and the Staff Manual respectively. Title pages will be prepared in manuscript.

Place	Date	Hour	Summary of Events and Information	Remarks and references to Appendices
BAILLEUL LES PERNES	May 1918 1st		Routine in Billets.	WD
"	2		"	WD
"	3		"	WD
"	4		The Regiment Paraded at 9am and marched to BOURBERS-SUR-CANCHE were it arrived the night.	WD
BOURBERS	5		The Regt moved to VILLERS L'HOPITAL.	WD
VILLERS L'HOPITAL	6		The Regt moved to CONTAY	WD
CONTAY	7		The Regt stood to at 1/2 hours notice from 6am to 8am	WD
"	8		" in Support to III Corps	WD
"	9		" to 6am, remainder 1 day on 3 hours	WD
"	10		"	WD
"	11		The Regiment found a party of 150 O.R. to diggings at HENNENCOURT.	WD
"	12		The Regt stood to from 5am.	WD
"	13		"	WD
"	14		"	WD
"	15		"	WD
"	16		"	WD

Army Form C. 2118.

WAR DIARY
or
INTELLIGENCE SUMMARY.
(Erase heading not required.)

3rd Dragoon Guards
17th May 1917

Instructions regarding War Diaries and Intelligence Summaries are contained in F. S. Regs., Part II. and the Staff Manual respectively. Title pages will be prepared in manuscript.

Place	Date	Hour	Summary of Events and Information	Remarks and references to Appendices
CONTAY.	May 1917 17		The Regt moved from CONTAY to BELLOY-SUR-SOMME	WD
BELLOY.	18		The G.O.C. inspected all Officers chargers	WD
	19		The Corps Commander distributed Ribbands on Bde Parade *	*List of Recipients attached
	20		Routine in Billets	WD
	21			
	22			
	23		2/Lieut A. R. Holmes proceed to 9th Cavl	WD
	24		Routine in Billets	WD
	25		" " "	WD
	26		" " "	WD
	27		Routine in Billets	WD
	28		" " "	WD
	29		" " "	WD
	30		" " "	WD
	31		The Regt marched to BEHENCOURT and bivouacked in Wood.	WD WD

W A Grimshaw
Capt.
Adjutant 3rd Dragoon Guards

WAR DIARY
or
INTELLIGENCE SUMMARY.

(Erase heading not required.)

Army Form C. 2118.

3rd Dragoon Guards

Vol 41

Place	Date	Hour	Summary of Events and Information	Remarks and references to Appendices
BEHENCOURT	June/18 1		Routine in Camp, Rgt Regt at this period was in support to Rt III Corps at BEHENCOURT.	MAQ
"	2		"	
"	3		G.O.C. 6th Cav. Bde. carried out an inspection of All horses in Rgt Regt.	MAQ
"	4		Working Party found by Regt for work on HENNENCOURT defences.	MAQ
"	5		Routine in Camp.	
"	6		G.O.C. 6th Cav. Bde. inspected the Regt in marching order, and afterwards expressed his appreciation in an order to the Regt.	MAQ
"	7		Work on Hennencourt defences.	MAQ
"	8		Routine in Camp.	MAQ
"	9		"	MAQ
"	10		" — Work on Hennencourt defences	MAQ
"	11		"	MAQ
"	12		"	MAQ
"	13		"	MAQ
BELLOY-SUR-SOMME	14		The Bde. moved from BEHENCOURT to BELLOY-SUR-SOMME.	MAQ

WAR DIARY or INTELLIGENCE SUMMARY.

3rd Dragoon Guards.

Army Form C. 2118.

(Erase heading not required.)

Place	Date	Hour	Summary of Events and Information	Remarks and references to Appendices
BELLOY-SUR-SOMME.	June 15.		Routine in Billets.	
"	16.		D. 19866. T.S.M. Logan awarded the L.S.&G.C. Medal.	
"	17.		A Bde Signalling Scheme was carried out.	
"	18.		Routine in Billets.	
"	19.		"	
"	20.		"	
"	21.		"	
"	22.		Dismounted Sports	
"	23.		A.R.A. Competition at Bouchon.	
"	24.		Routine in Billets.	
"	25.		The Bde moved to Le Mesge Area.	
LE MESGE.	26.		Routine in Billets.	
"	27.		"	
"	28.		Horses inspected by A.D.V.S.	
"	29.		Routine in Billets. Staff Ride for Officers	
"	30.			

WAR DIARY

INTELLIGENCE SUMMARY.
(Erase heading not required.)

Army Form C. 2118.

July 1918
3rd Dragoon Guards

Shear. I.

Place	Date	Hour	Summary of Events and Information	Remarks and references to Appendices
LE MESGE	July 1918 1.		Routine in Billets.	MAG
	2			
	3			MAG
	4			
	5			
	6			
	7			
	8		A.D.V.S. Inspected the horses of the Regt.	MAG
	9		11. O.R. and 6 Chargers joined from ABBEVILLE.	MAG
	10		Routine in Billets.	MAG
	11			MAG
	12			MAG
	13		Bde. Sports postponed owing to rain.	MAG
	14		1 Officer and 7 O.R. joined from Abbeville.	MAG
	15		Routine in Billets.	MAG
	16			
	17			MAG
	18			
	19			
	20			MAG
	21		50. O.R. joined C.C.R.C. from Base.	MAG
	22		Routine in Billets.	MAG
	23		Bde. Tbraud Sports.	MAG
	24		Routine in Billets.	MAG
	25		Bde. Horse Show. Rear H.Q. 2nd in M.D.	MAG MAG
	26		Routine in Billets	MAG
	27			MAG
	28			MAG
	29			MAG
	30			MAG
	31			MAG

H.A. Grinstead
Capt.
Adjutant 3rd Dragoon Guards.

WAR DIARY or INTELLIGENCE SUMMARY.

Army Form C. 2118.

Sheet No I 6/3
3.D.G.

Vol 43

Place	Date	Hour	Summary of Events and Information	Remarks and references to Appendices
LE MESGE	1918 Aug 1		Routine in Billets.	WD
"	2		" " "	WD
"	3		" " "	WD
"	4		" " "	WD
"	5		" " "	WD
"	6		The Regt. moved to PONT DE METZ at 10.30 pm in order to take part in the attack of Aug 8th	WD
FIELD	7		} Active Operations. See Appendix A	WD
	8			
	9			
	10			
FOUENCAMPS	11		The Regt returned to FOUENCAMPS, leaving LA FOLIE at 5.30 pm	WD
			Casualties during period of Operation. K. W. Missing	
	12		B Echelon joined Regt at FOUENCAMPS 1. 2. 1.	WD
	13		Routine in Billets. - Horse Inspection -	WD
	14		" " "	WD
LE MESGE	15		Regt marched back to LE MESGE.	WD
	16		Routine in Billets	WD
	17		Training.	WD
	18		Divine Service.	WD

APPENDIX "A"

3rd DRAGOON GUARDS
DIARY OF OPERATIONS
August 8th......to....August 11th 1918.

Reference AMIENS MAP. 1/100,000.

August 8th. Zero hour 4.20 a.m.
The 6th Cavalry Brigade was then in support to the 3rd Cavalry Division, 3 miles East of LONGEAU.

6.0 a.m.   Brigade moved to CACHY.
10.0 a.m. Brigade moved to BOGREMONT Wood.
11.0 a.m. Brigade moved to the high ground S of IGNAUCOURT via DEMUIN.

Reports received that the Canadian Cavalry Brigade had captured BEAUCOURT, and that the 7th Cavalry Brigade was held up by heavy M.G. Fire from the high ground N.E. of LE QUESNEL. The Royals were sent off to reinforce the 7th Brigade.

2.0 p.m.   Message received that the Royals were in VRELY and WARVILLERS, and the 3rd Dragoon Guards were ordered to prolong and cover the right flank of the Royals, The 10th Hussars being in support, this order was subsequently cancelled, and the Brigade concentrated on the high ground S of CAIX at 4.0 p.m.

5.30 p.m. Orders were received for the Brigade to hold a line in support of the Infantry, and to join up with the 7th Brigade on the right and the 1st Cavalry Division on the left. The line held running S from CAIX along the QUESNEL Road.
The Royals and 10th Hussars found the outposts the 3rd Dragoon Guards being in support.
The Brigade bivouacked for the night in the Valley S of CAIX.

August 9th.
11.0 a.m. Brigade moved to the Valley of the LUCE between CAIX and CAYEUX. The 3rd Cavalry Division being in Corps reserve.

August 10th. The 3rd Cavalry Division was ordered to relieve the 1st and 2nd Cavalry Divisions who were co-operating with the Infantry. The 6th Cavalry Brigade was allotted the Sector from the Amiens - ROYE road at BOUCHOIR to a line VRELY - FOUQUESCOURT - HATTENCOURT. The 7th Brigade being on the left of the 6th Brigade.

5.0 a.m.   C. Squadron 3rd Dragoon Guards (Captain A.B.P.L.VINCENT M.C.) and Captain MILES Squadron Royals moved forward, Vincent on the right and MILES on the left, to gain touch with the Infantry.

5.20 a.m. The Brigade moved forward to a position between VRELY and BEAUFORT.

10.30 a.m. The 3rd Dragoon Guards moved to FOLIES, The Royals to WARVILLERS. Brigade Hd Qrs and 10th Hussars to the W of FOLIES.

11.30 a.m. C Squadron moved forward across Country to LE QUESNOY but owing to the broken state of the ground and heavy shelling of the Village was ordered back to FOLIES by the C.O.
The Infantry had by this time come to a standstill in front of DAMERY and PARVILLERS, The Country being very much broken up by old trench systems and wire. Hopeless for Cavalry action.

2.40 p.m. On information being received that ANDECHY had been taken by the French B. Squadron 3rd Dragoon Guards moved down the ROYE Road with orders to be ready to take advantage of any opportunities that might arise.
                                                                either
A & C Squadrons moving to LE QUESNOY with a view to supporting B Squadron or moving by road to either PARVILLERS or DAMERY.

4.0 p.m.   The Canadian Cavalry Brigade tried to gallop down the the ROYE Road but coming under Heavy M.G. fire were unable to advance.

(Sheet 2.)
August 10th continued
The 10th Hussars were ordered up in support of the Canadian Brigade

9.30 p.m. The Brigade was ordered to concentrate N of FOLIES. Situation being, The French on the right of the ROYE Road was held up by Hill 100, and our Infantry were unable to advance E of a line drawn through the D of DAMERY thence through the S H of LE QUESNOY and the LL of PARVILLERS.

The Brigade bivouacked for the night at FOLIES.

August 11th.

5.30 p.m. The Brigade moved back to FOUENCAMPS.

WAR DIARY
INTELLIGENCE SUMMARY
(Erase heading not required.)

Army Form C. 2118.

Sheet 1

3ʳᵈ Dragoon Guards

Place	Date	Hour	Summary of Events and Information	Remarks and references to Appendices
FREVENT	1918 Sept 1		Training commenced S.E. of FREVENT.	WAG
"	2		" " " "	WAG
"	3		" " " "	WAG
"	4			
"	5			
"	6		Orders received for Regt to move to 16th WAIL area.	WAG
"	7		The Regt marched to WAIL leaving at 9am.	WAG
"	8		3ʳᵈ Cav. Div. places in G.H.Q Reserve.	WAG
WAIL	9		Training carried out in WAIL area	WAG
"	10		" " " " "	WAG
"	11		" " " " "	WAG
"	12		" " " " "	WAG
"	13		" " " " "	WAG
"	14		" " " " "	WAG
"	15		Orders recd for Regt to take part in Corps Scheme. The Regt, less A2 and B Echelon proceed to GRIGNY	WAG
"	16		to take part in Scheme.	WAG
"	17		Manoeuvres carried out in AUTHIE area. e-i-e	WAG

"2° Strafon Guards"

Army Form C. 2118.

WAR DIARY
INTELLIGENCE SUMMARY
(Erase heading not required.)

Instructions regarding War Diaries and Intelligence Summaries are contained in F.S. Regs., Part II. and the Staff Manual respectively. Title pages will be prepared in manuscript.

Place	Date	Hour	Summary of Events and Information	Remarks and references to Appendices
WAIL	Sept 1918 18		The Regiment returned to WAIL.	WD
"	19		The Regiment marched to a new area, Gd & Pt BOURET.	WD
"	20		Training in Gd BOURET.	WD
"	21		" " " "	WD
"	22		" " " "	WD
"	23		" " " "	WD
"	24		Regiment prepared to move.	WD
"	25		Regiment marched to LOUVINCOURT, when it went into billets.	WD
LOUVINCOURT	26		The Regiment continued its march to MEAULTE, an went into bivouac.	WD
MEAULTE	27		Bde moved to concentration area about HEM.	WD
HEM	28		The Regiment remained in bivouac during 28th.	WD
"	29		The Regiment then Bde later moved to BIHECOURT.	WD
BIHECOURT	30		The Regiment stood to at BIHECOURT.	WD

W. A. Grimshaw
Capt
Adjutant 2° Dragoon Guards

Army Form C. 2118.

3 DRAGOON GUARDS 6/3

Nov 4

WAR DIARY
or
INTELLIGENCE SUMMARY.
(Erase heading not required.)

Place	Date	Hour	Summary of Events and Information	Remarks and references to Appendices
BIHECOURT.	1918 Oct 1.		The Regiment remained on 4 hour notice at BIHECOURT.	WBG
	2.		The Regiment moved to a position of readiness first to BELLENGLISE but returned to BIHECOURT later owing to enemy counter attack having developed (see Appendix A).	WBG
	3,4,5,6,7,8,9,10,11,12		See Appendix A attached	
ELINCOURT.	13.		The Regt remained at ELINCOURT 4. OR reinforcements and 48 OR already on strength joining W|LT 52 know.	WBG
BANTOUZELLE	14.		The Regiment moved to BANTOUZELLE and spent the night in Sugar factory	WBG

August 1918.

Army Form C. 2118.

3 Dragoon Guards

WAR DIARY
or
INTELLIGENCE SUMMARY.

Sheet No 2.

(Erase heading not required.)

Instructions regarding War Diaries and Intelligence Summaries are contained in F.S. Regs., Part II. and the Staff Manual respectively. Title pages will be prepared in manuscript.

Place	Date	Hour	Summary of Events and Information	Remarks and references to Appendices
LE MESGE.	19		Training carried out round billets.	
	20			
	21		The Bde marched from LE.MESGE to MONTRELET.	
MONTRELET	22		The Bde remained at MONTRELET.	
"	23		"	
"	24		"	
"	25		Bde marched to LE PONCHEL, and was placed on 2½ hrs notice	
LE PONCHEL	26		Bde marched to SERICOURT Area, Regt being billeted in SERICOURT	
SERICOURT	27		Regt placed on 2½ hrs notice to move	
"	28		Bde stood to at ½ hr notice to move	
"	29			
"	30			
"	31			

W.A Grimshaw
Capt.
Adjutant. 3rd Dragoon Guards.

Army Form C. 2118.

WAR DIARY
or
INTELLIGENCE SUMMARY.
(Erase heading not required.)

3rd DRAGOON GDS

Place	Date	Hour	Summary of Events and Information	Remarks and references to Appendices
MANANCOURT	Oct 18 1st		The Regiment entrained the march and went into camp at Manancourt, occupying for the most part old German huts. M.O. R.'s previously reported as "missing" rejoined.	
"	16		M.O. R.'s previously reported as "missing" rejoined. 42 O.R. & horses rejoined from Base.	1093
"	17		Improvement of Billets.	
"	18		12 O.R. reinforcements received.	
"	19		Improvement of Billets.	
"	20		Bde. Tactical Exercise.	x 2/Lt L. Walker.
"	21		Stables commenced to be built. 7 Officers joined from England.	Mr W. Black. M T. Koller. Mr M.E. Longbottom. M C.E. Harwood. 2/Lt E.K. Ford. Mr H.H. Peard.
"	22		Building of Stables continued.	
"	23		"	P.O.W. 34 O.R. joined (including 29 O.R. ⊙ 2/Lt Royal) Regina which were left at P.O.W.R.P. 2/Lt P.S.R. Perrott.
"	24		"	
"	25		"	
"	26		"	
"	27		6 O.R. joined from Base.	
"	28		Stables completed.	
"	29		All Ranks tested in Gas.	
"	30		A.D.V.S. inspected horses of Regt.	
"	31		G.O.C. 6th Cav Bde inspected B Sqdn in Marching Drill, Watering Order	

[signatures]

3/rd DRAGOON GUARDS

Narrative of events from September 23rd to Octr 12th 1918

Sept 23rd. The Regiment which was billetted near FREVENT, was warned that the Brigade would take part in Active Operations.

Sept 25th. The Regiment moved from Gd BOURET near FREVENT to LOUVENCOURT moving at night.

Sept 26th. Remained at LOUVENCOURT during the day but moved to a bivouac Area about MEAULTE during the night.

Sept 27th. The Regiment left MEAULTE and moved to an Area between HEM and CLERY where it went into Camp.

Sept 28th. Remained in Camp at CLERY.

Sept 29th. Received orders that Brigade would be on 3 hours notice. Later, orders were received that the Brigade would move at 13.45 hours.
The Regiment then marched to BIHECOURT and were bivouaced at night just West of the X Roads. Rain fell heavily all night.

Sept 30th. Regiment ordered to be ready to move by 5.45 a.m, but later was placed on 3 hours notice.

Octr 1st. Regiment stood to at BIHECOURT.

Oct 2d. The Regiment left BIHECOURT at 09.30 and moved to an assembly area on the CANAL BANK just West of BELLENGLISE. About midday news was received that the Germans had delivered a heavy counter attack and had succeeded in driving in our advanced outposts in the MONTBREHAIN Sector. In consequence of this the Brigade was ordered to move back to BIHECOURT.

Oct 3d. Orders were again received for the Brigade to concentrate at BELLENGLISE. The Regiment therefore left BIHECOURT at 10.30 hours and arrived in assembly area about 11.15 hours. About 15.00 hours report was received from the Brigade Observation Officer who was in RAMICOURT that the Germans had been seen retiring for the high ground S.E. of MONBREHAIN. The Brigade was therefore ordered up to PRESELLES, 3rd Dragoon Guards being advanced Guard to the Brigade. The Regiment moved forward on a 2 Squadron frontage A on the right B on the left. Much difficulty was experienced in wire. On arrival at H.17.b. the Regiment dismounted, the Commanding Officer going forward to reconnoitre the enemy's position, shortly afterwards he was joined by G.O.C. 6th Cavalry Brigade who decided that no further mounted action was possible, owing to enemy holdinh MONBREHAIN and the high ground on the S.E. in strength.
As the Infantry seemed disprganised and had no Officers with the it was decided to hold the line with the Infantry but scarcely had the line been taken up when orders were received for the Regiment less 1 Squadron to move back to PONTRUET.
A. Squadron was ordered to remain at MAGNY LA FOSSE under orders of the 46th Division with orders to send out Patrols at dawn to find out the situation on the 9th Corps front. During the afternoon the Valley in which the horses were was heavily shelled with H.E. and Blue Cross shell gas and there were very many casualties.
CASUALTIES.   O.Rs Killed 2.   O.Rs Wounded. 13   Horses 59.

Sheet. 2.

Octr 4th. A. Squadron rejoined the Regiment about 4 p.m. having been relieved by a Squadron of the 1st Royal Dragoons.
One of the Patrols which were sent out by A. Squadron in the morning under 2/Lieut C.H. Priestley had all its horses shot and had to return on foot.

Octr 5th. The Regiment paraded at 7. a.m. and moved back to TREFCON where of the horses were able to be got under cover.

Octr 6th. Remained at TREFCON. The Commanding Officer inspected all horses of the Regiment.

Octr 7th. Regiment warned that the Brigade would move at an early hour to an assembly area S.W. of MAGNY LA FOSSE.

Octr 8th. The Regiment paraded at 03.45 hours and moved to an Area S.W. of MAGNY LA FOSSE arriving about 7. a.m. At about 10.00 hours, orders were received that the Brigade would move in support of the 1st Cavalry Division which was reported to be in action about TREMONT, accordingly Brigade moved to a position about 1000 yards West of ESTREES and thence to an Area about 800 yards S.E. of ESTREES. The Divisional and Brigade Headquarters being established on the main ESTREES - Le CATEAU Road.
C. Squadron had been sent from Magny LA FOSSE to Estrees earlier in the morning to act as Escort to Corps Commander.
The Brigade received orders to return to the Area S.W. of MAGNY LA FOSSE at 6.30. C. Squadron was also ordered to rejoin the Regiment.

Octr 9th. Moved at daybreak to BEAUREVOIR. The 3rd Cavalry Division being leading Division. Reports received stated that the enemy had retired, accordingly the 6th Brigade moved forward to MARETZ with the Canadians North of the Main Road. The Royals went forward but were held up by fire from MAURIOS and HONNECHEY. At 13.30 the 3rd Dragoon Guards were ordered to move to BUSIGNY and after crossing the railway to work round HONNECHEY from the S.E. This was done under heavy M.G. and Field Gun Fire.
A. Squadron did advance Guard Squadron to the Regiment the remainder of the Regiment following in line of Troop Columns well opened out. By 14.40 the Village of HONNECHEY and the high ground at P.25.c. had been captured. The village was heavily shelled throughout the remainder of the day causing many casualties to men and horses. As no report had been received as to whether REUMONT was ours or not A. & B. Squadrons under Captain N.K. Worthington M.C. were ordered to REUMONT. At 1630 hours Reumont was reported clear of the enemy. The G.O.C. 6th Brigade therefore ordered the whole Brigade to move to REUMONT with a view to passing through it and seizing the high ground West of LE CATEAU. Just as the Brigade was starting off orders were received from the Division that the 7th Brigade had been ordered to move on final Objective. Orders were then received for the Brigade to Bivouac for the night A.& B. Sqdn being relieved in REUMONT by Infantry.

CASUALTIES.
Lieut V. Oakley Brown. Killed
Lt: Col: C.L. Rome D.S.O. Wounded
Captain H.P. Holt. "
Lieut B.H. Osmaston "
Lieut E.A.L. Kittle Died of wounds.
Killed Other Ranks....2. Wounded Other Ranks...29.
Missing Other Ranks....2. Horses....90.

Octr 10th. The Regiment marched at 05.00 to an Area West of TROISVILLES where Major J.T. Gibbs took over Command of the Regiment.
As 7th Brigade were unable to cross the River SELLE, the Brigade was ordered back to MONTIGNY where it bivouaced the night.

Octr 11th. At 13.30 the Regiment march to ELINCOURT.

Octr 12th. Remained in ELINCOURT.

WAR DIARY
INTELLIGENCE SUMMARY. Sheet I.

Army Form C. 2118.
3d Dragoon Gds

Place	Date 1918 Nov.	Hour	Summary of Events and Information	Remarks and references to Appendices
MARETZCOURT	2		Routine in Billets. Bde Scheme carried out in direction of QUYENCOURT	WMG
"	3 4/5		Routine in Billets.	WMG
"	6		The Regt marched to MARQUION, Rain fell heavily during the day - and night.	WMG
"	7		March continued to ESQUERCHIN, where Regt billets the night. Route, via DOUAI.	WMG
"	8		March continued to LOUVIL. Escort Troop to G.O.C. 3d Cav. Division ordered to join Division.	WMG
"	9		In billets at LOUVIL.	WMG
"	10		The Regt moved to VAULX-LEZ-TOURNAI.	WMG
"	11		The Regt moved to Bde rendez-vous at GAURAIN RAMECROIX. Bde given orders to seize the line ATH - CHIÈVRES, & in consequence 3d Dragoon Gds were ordered to advance on	WMG

WAR DIARY
INTELLIGENCE SUMMARY

Army Form C. 2118.
3 Dragon Gds

Place	Date	Hour	Summary of Events and Information	Remarks and references to Appendices
Lies.	11.	9.30	On the night the Royals and the left. X.R.H. in support. The Regt was ordered to advance on a two Sqdn frontage, A on the right, C on the left. The Regt moved off at 0900, along the main ATH–LEUZE–TOURNAI road. The road was packed with returning civilian prisoners and refugees who spoke of the great confusion behind the enemy lines. On arrival	
		10.20	at the Western entrance to LEUZE the Bde was met by Major S.G. Howes who stated that the town was over. The Bde then hurried with its leaders in LEUZE. The streets were packed with people and flags were hanging out of every house. The Bde O.C. official notification were received at 1100 was "Hostilities	
		11.00	All the Trumpeters in the Bde were brought into the Squad and sounded the Cease fire at 1100. A Bath of the K.O. Lancaster Regt was also on parade in the Square.	

Army Form C. 2118.

3º Seaforth

WAR DIARY
or
INTELLIGENCE SUMMARY.
(Erase heading not required.)

Instructions regarding War Diaries and Intelligence Summaries are contained in F. S. Regs., Part II and the Staff Manual respectively. Title pages will be prepared in manuscript.

Place	Date	Hour	Summary of Events and Information	Remarks and references to Appendices
LEUZE	11		The Bde Hd moved our of LEUZE in order to clear the road, and at 1430 moved to VAULX-LEZ-TOURNAI.	
VAULX	12.		The Regt moved to HASMES.	MM
HASMES	13.		Regt HQ Hd Bde moved from Parr to advance guard to Troops entering Germany. Consequently all swords, log chains etc ordered to be burnished, and turn up to be as well turned out as possible.	MM
HASMES	14 15 16 17		Burnishing.	MMS MM
	18	abr 10 am	Regt moved to GRATY, passing through the outposts at the Regt marched to WENNUEYERES, and VIRGINAL SAMME and took up a line of outposts E of their place.	MM
	19.		in agar- to WENNUEYERES respectively the officers to the Regt	MM

WAR DIARY

INTELLIGENCE SUMMARY

Army Form C. 2118.

B. Drapor?

4.

(Erase heading not required.)

Instructions regarding War Diaries and Intelligence Summaries are contained in F. S. Regs., Part II. and the Staff Manual respectively. Title pages will be prepared in manuscript.

Place	Date	Hour	Summary of Events and Information	Remarks and references to Appendices
HENNUYERES.	19.		To attend a reception at the Town Hall, accordingly this was done, the Mayor reading our an address of welcome to the four British Troops to enter their village. Major d.T. Gills replied on behalf of the Regt.	WMS
"	20.		Remained at HENNUYERES. Cavalry Corps Concert Party gave a concert to the Regt. at VIRGINAL SAMME. Several British Prisoners of War came into our lines having been abandoned by the Germans.	WMS
	21.		The Regiment continued the advance and reached an outpost position E of Mont St Guibert being in touch with the 1st Cav Div on right and Royals on left.	WMS
MONT. ST. GUIBERT.	22.		Advanced continued to NANRET. 2 large Gun Parks at EGHEZEE as well as motor lorries etc. A Wireless message had previously been received saying that a guard must be left behind. Hinrquard was found.	WMS

Army Form C. 2118.

3 Dragoon Gds

(5)

WAR DIARY
or
INTELLIGENCE SUMMARY.
(Erase heading not required.)

Instructions regarding War Diaries and Intelligence Summaries are contained in F. S. Regs., Part II. and the Staff Manual respectively. Title pages will be prepared in manuscript.

Place	Date	Hour	Summary of Events and Information	Remarks and references to Appendices
HANRET.	23.		Regt remained at HANRET.	WD
	24.		Orders received to the effect that 1st Cav. Div to my move continue its advance, consequently Gloster Regt moved to Dhuy	WD
DHUY.	25.		Move to Dhuy carried out.	WD
	26.		Infantry passed through	WD
	27.		" " "	WD
	28.		Routine in Billets.	WD
	29.		" " "	WD
	30.		" " "	WD

H.A.Gunishaw.
Capt.
Adjutant. 3rd Dragoon Gds.

WAR DIARY
or
INTELLIGENCE SUMMARY.

Army Form C. 2118.

2nd Grenville Shul 1

Place	Date 1918	Hour	Summary of Events and Information	Remarks and references to Appendices
DHUY	Dec 1		Routine in Billets. Papers dealing with demobilization received.	WAS
"	2			WAS
"	3			WAS
"	4			WAS
"	5			WAS
"	6		Routine in Billets.	WAS
"	7			WAS
"	8			WAS
"	9			
"	10		The Regiment moved to ANTHET, just N of HUY and billeted there.	WAS
ANTHET	11		The Reg't remained at further billeting parties went fwd to permanent winter area about ST GEORGES.	WAS
ST GEORGES	12		Regiment moved to ST GEORGES, DOMMARTIN and GLEIXHE.	WAS
	13		Improvement of Billets. Many men away on leave.	WAS

Army Form C. 2118.

WAR DIARY
or
INTELLIGENCE SUMMARY. Sheet 2
(Erase heading not required.)

Instructions regarding War Diaries and Intelligence Summaries are contained in F. S. Regs., Part II. and the Staff Manual respectively. Title pages will be prepared in manuscript.

Place	Date 12/18	Hour	Summary of Events and Information	Remarks and references to Appendices
ST GEORGES	Dec 22		Demobilization Commenced. 7 Cairmen and 2 Demobilizers	WAS
"	23		Sent to England.	
	24		Routine.	WAS
	25		16 Men to England	WAS
	26		Xmas Day. Comdg Officer visits each Sqdn Mess and Sqdn Mess Dinner and Guests	WAS
	27			WAS
	28		Routine in Billets	
	29			
	30			
	31			

W.A. Grimshaw
Capt
Adjutant 3rd Dragoon Gds

3 Dragoon Guards Army Form C.2118.
Sheet I

WAR DIARY
or
INTELLIGENCE SUMMARY.
(Erase heading not required.)

Instructions regarding War Diaries and Intelligence Summaries are contained in F. S. Regs., Part II. and the Staff Manual respectively. Title pages will be prepared in manuscript.

Place	Date	Hour	Summary of Events and Information	Remarks and references to Appendices
St George	Jan 1st 1919 – 31st Jan 1919		Owing to Demobilization nothing of importance occured.	Nil

W.A. Chambers
Capt.
Adjutant. 3rd Dragoon Guards

www.ingramcontent.com/pod-product-compliance
Lightning Source LLC
Chambersburg PA
CBHW081525160426
43191CB00011B/1685